SELFISH

Also by ALBERT GOLDBARTH

ALBERT
GOLDBARTH

POEMS

SELFISH

Graywolf Press

This publication is made possible, in part, by the voters of Minnesota through a Minnesota State Arts Board Operating Support grant, thanks to a legislative appropriation from the arts and cultural heritage fund, and through grants from the National Endowment for the Arts and the Wells Fargo Foundation Minnesota. Significant support has also been provided by Target, the McKnight Foundation, Amazon.com, and other generous contributions from foundations, corporations, and individuals. To these organizations and individuals we offer our heartfelt thanks.

Published by Graywolf Press
250 Third Avenue North, Suite 600
Minneapolis, Minnesota 55401

www.graywolfpress.org

Published in the United States of America

ISBN 978-1-55597-708-5

2 4 6 8 9 7 5 3 1
First Graywolf Printing, 2015

Library of Congress Control Number: 2014960036

Cover design: Kyle G. Hunter

Cover art: Ancient cave paintings in Patagonia, Argentina. Photo © elnavegante. Used with the permission of Shutterstock.

for Skyler

"My Love has made me selfish. I cannot exist without you."
—John Keats, in a letter to Fanny Brawne

The bliss which God unchangingly enjoys in his neverending self-contemplation is the Good after which all other things yearn.

—from *The Great Chain of Being,* Arthur O. Lovejoy

It has been
absolutely

fascinating
being me.

A unique
privilege

—from "Memoir," Dennis O'Driscoll

. . . and she reviewed, as if it were an avenue of great edifices, the progress of her own self along her own past.

—from *Orlando,* Virginia Woolf

I contain multitudes (**Walt Whitman**); I think I have three souls (**Kenneth Koch**).

I'm Nobody! Who are you? Are you Nobody, too?

—Emily Dickinson

During more than three years exploring South America aboard the *Beagle,* Darwin collected 27 species of mice, including a bright-eyed specimen he named after himself.

—*National Geographic, 125 Years of Great Explorations*

The problem, of course, is that when it comes to life and death, we don't think about statistical significance and sample groups of 1,000, we think of sample groups of one—and we're the only member.

—from "The Angelina Effect" in *Time* (May 27, 2013), Jeffrey Kluger and Alice Park

I don't think it's particularly selfish not to want to die.

—from *The Stars Like Dust,* Isaac Asimov

I think he'd have hated the selfie. He did not want love as opiate or ego-massage. He wanted something that would help us live on earth.

—Jesse Nathan, on poet Edward Dorn

He questions Silicon Valley's assumption that the quantified self is the truest self, that we can find a deeper verity in empirically accurate, supported data than we can in the stories we tell about ourselves.

—review of a book by Evegny Morozov in *Time* (April 8, 2013)

New powers, new allies, a new plan to make myself what I should always have been, master of worlds!

—Ul Quorn, the Magician of Mars and nemesis of Captain Future,

from *The Solar Invasion,* Manly Wade Wellman

I have spent my whole life doing what I love.

—from "The Buff-Chested Grouse," Robert Bly

He had taken bypaths, and crossed many fields, and changed his course several times, in case of pursuit; but now, feeling by this time safe from recapture, and the sun smiling brightly on him, and all nature joining in a chorus of approval to the song of self-praise that his own heart was singing to him, he almost danced along the road in his satisfaction. . . . He was giddy and ecstatic. He went skating down a looping bridge of magnetic flux. He danced madly in the midst of a sputtering cloud of ions. He ducked his erratic way through the core of an exploding galaxy. He ran a race with the surging radiation that flared out of a nova. He somersaulted through a field of pulsars.

—mash-up of Kenneth Grahame *(The Wind in the Willows)*

and Clifford D. Simak *(Project Pope)*

CONTENTS

Lineage(s)

Everyday Life on Planet Albert

Selfish

Other Lives

Paintings, Poems, Surveys, Songs, and Other Lyric Flights

LINEAGE(S)

Snow

Is anybody flabbergasted anymore?
Does anyone get the willies or the heebie-jeebies?
Is anyone floored? Or saying "Great Caesar's ghost!"
Does anyone have his socks knocked off six ways from Sunday?
Language is ever being born, is struggling out
of some cultural pupal case and drying its wings.
Hey, I was there to witness when "shizzle" and "phat"
undertook their initial flights. Of course, the law is
language needs to die, to make room—like anyone.
"Carbon footprint" yes and "carbon paper" no.
"Phlebotomy." "Manufactory." "Ceinture."
Good-bye. And names. Lavonda lately, Tayvon lately.
But Fannie? Irving? There they are
on my parents' stones, under a veiling snowfall.

Lineage

In Jewish tradition the rule seems to be that a name is not
only powerful but singular: one soul per name. A newborn
is never named for a living family member: the soul might
have to choose between them.

My wife is online, branching back in time
through a US census genealogy site, a little
like astronomy: the stars are dead and yet
their light is examinable on Earth.

At some point, the blood of the Cherokee
enters the stream . . . at another, one couple
owned slaves . . . a father and son were lynched
by the KKK for holding anti-secessionist views . . .
Arvonia . . . Ophra . . . Zaphora . . .
haughty, drafty 16th century castle life. . . .
It may be that the infant Moses,
swaddled in a basket in the bulrushes,
simply appeared from out of nowhere, unconnected
to a family tree . . . well, not my wife!

⁓

And she enters "Goldbarth," but everything stops
for me at my grandparents' generation. What
a holocaust does.

That night, I have a dream, a kind of postmodern dream:
I dream I'm sleeping. My wife is sleeping.
And as we sleep, her laptop keeps on doing its virtual
retroprogressional business, branching back
along the central river, back against the current
of its tributaries, feathering, fractaling, back
through the veins and the capillaries,
the source, the bud, and I awake

confused and enhanced and seminal,
having the eyes of something
just stumped out of the waters, learning to first breathe air.

⁓

A spaceman from the future (and when I speak with him later
he specifies the future is 2515 AD) is windmill-armed
in fisticuffs with a coonskin-capped and buckskin-fringed
frontiersman straight from Booneville (who's no slouch
at trading haymakers), and they seem to be determining
who earns the right to accompany Miss Silver Spandex (later
I'll learn she's a self-created superfemmefatale she calls
Mysteria) to the costume ball; across the hall
a World-War-IIesque Wonder Woman appears, and
Captain Nanobot from the 22nd century, they join
this popcult free-for-all—this achronological
dice-and-resplice American shmooshed-up evernow.
No wonder the laws of counterbalance require my wife
establishing a history of sequential links.

⁓

Oh I *know* how corny it sounds, but
there are mornings I wake and turn to see my wife
asleep . . . mysterious,
in her faraway dreams; unaccountably
here . . . and I think of when my friend Delora,
hiking through a silent, solitary stretch
of Ohio forest, suddenly
chanced upon a shard of what her daughter Rae would call
"a falling star," still faintly radiating
the heat of its journey.
                                        We think that water
came to Earth originally on meteorites. We think
the code of life itself may have fallen to Earth
from out of the void, from Up There, where the stars
are the beginning of everybody's genealogy.

                                  ∾

"My wife," "My Cherokee shaman ancestor,"
"My silver spandex miniskirt I stitched with sixteen
faux-pearl buttons for all of the planets I've visited":
constructs; "tenure," "poems," "my children," ways we have
of trying to hammer our lives so deeply into the planet,
time can't dislodge us. Yes, we know it doesn't work
—my father and mother are less than dew
around their memorial stones—and yet that doesn't
stop us from accumulating the details. Here: my mother
nightly rinsed the gunk from the poodle's eyes.
My father wizarded homemade blackberry brandy every year.
My grandpa Albert was dead before I was born, or
I'd be otherwise named. Jews know how terribly fragile
breath is. Sunlight is starlight dying up closer.

On the Way

But by the time the urologist said "benign"

I'd already been translucent for over a week, half here
and half resigned to the air
and the magnetism and the amino acids
of everywhere else—my heart
with its signature whisper and fist, already
half planning on pouring back completely
into the general fund.

Even now, on the simple drive up 35
from Wichita to Kansas City, I'm thinking in terms
of losing one's self, I'm thinking
 of an arc that starts at Ellis Island, 1898,

and of my grandparents, who are leaning
on the rail of the ferry as it hops in place on the water,
itching to be let loose for Manhattan—lost in the thought
of a future too big for their heads to contain. This couple,
eager to pick the thick-packed, throat-roll fat of Old World Yiddish
from their teeth, and spit it into the smeary Hudson, eager to trade it
for a language free of cholera and the Tsar. Or if not eager, still
they understand the inevitable: these herring-belching,
heavy-hatted and black-robed orthodoxauruses, starting
already, by a food choice here, a jump rope singsong there, to die out

into their own children and their children's children,
space race, iPhone, mall. And *why* I'm thinking
in these terms . . . ?—perhaps this other rolling ocean,
or metaphorical "ocean," or anyway late-spring grasslands hills
around this Midwest highway, that were also someone's voyage.
All the Way to California! read one conestoga wagon's side; although
there were plenty who gave up here in Kansas, and made lives

on just such plump ripe hills as these. The culmination
of that grand American narrative is singing from my radio,

this latest eighteen-year-old überwondergirlie diva
with the blonde dreads and the street cred
and the anglo-afro-euro-latino sexed-together butter-skin
that's equally the live apotheosis of the promise of this country

and a mass grave for the individuation that needed to disappear
on the way. Whatever, her boogie-and-Beethoven bootie-beat
is mucho inescapably infectious, and my own voice is a karaoke trickle now
that joins the rushing current of her mega-money hit.
You hear me? Yipping out the window?
I'm not dead! And I'm not even close to dead,

so far as I can tell; but I was—in the lab
and the week that followed—on loan to the country of death.
I had a temporary visa there,
checking out the dead restaurants and dead places of worship:
would I apply to stay? would I be accepted?
would I blend in, wearing the "right" dead clothes,
and intoning the same dead slogans as my neighbors?
That's all past, as I've said. But a visit like that

is altering; you become your own souvenir.
That me is what I've packed to bring along
as I speed and sing and tremble a little and brush it away this afternoon
an hour out of Emporia now with Kansas City almost in sight,
across the deep greens and the graves
of the long, long road of assimilation.

Metonymy

She worked as a specialty fetish model
—feet—and also did mainstream modeling:
pedicure products, bunion relief. . . . Indeed
her feet were something like a Platonic ideal
of feet—and you may not be among the tribe
who'd dream of slipping those toes
("imperially slim," as E. A. Robinson says
in his "Richard Cory" poem) from out of their enshrinement
in outré six-inch stilettos and paying them
oral adoration, or among the artsy-minded
who could easily imagine a plaster cast of them
in a museum case amid the marble glories
of ancient Greece and Rome . . . but let's just say
her bank account wasn't imperiled. "Although

it's . . . *strange* to be valued in such a partite way,"
she said (one friend of hers did hands; another provided her neck,
as perfect as an architect's stencil, for jewelry shoots:
it had a full-time agent), "and sometimes
I think of my feet as being detached
from my body and set in a gilded frame,"
(I suppose the stanza above exists to be their verbal frame)
"and other times I fantasize" (maybe it's the "frame"
that brings to mind the artist?) "van Gogh's ear
as it floats away from the damage, out to sea,
where it thrives, as if in a nutritional bath, until a new
van Gogh begins to grow around it, and is cast on a beach,
and starts to create the astonishing sun-drunk paintings
of a new life." If he's landed in America

in 1876 he'll be able to walk to Philadelphia
and see the torch-bearing hand of the Statue of Liberty
—the height of a house—where it stands
in a pavilion at the Centennial Exhibition, with the feel
of a rebus-word divorced from the text
that would otherwise give it meaning. Completed,
she'll rise 151 feet: you crunch the math
for yourself, and figure how gigantic, this imposing and
unbodied hand. By the time my grandfather saw it
over the harbor, it was already seamlessly part
of the copper-green whole of her, in her statuary majesty.
Then he landed on Ellis Island—one more uprooted immigrant
looking to be transplanted. *Lost Jews, lost Jews.* And the promise
he saw in this sculptural flame . . . by now

we've squandered it, in lies, in tinsel images
(if our leaders really *did* know about the Pearl Harbor attack
in advance, and allowed it to happen, *then*
what?—etc.); but for Louie, escaping the Jew-muck
that the soldiers of the Tsar would have trampled him into,
escaping the hunger times and the fear-stink times,
this truly was (her official title) *Liberty
Lighting the World.* And so years later, now with a business
he owned, and a woman he loved, and children, and
gefilte fish whenever he desired—with a life—he asked
permission to make a symbolic gesture of gratitude,
and boarded a ferry for Bedloe's Island, and stepped ashore,
squinting into the sun, and for just one minute he kneeled there
and he worshipped at her feet.

Liquid

All told, the moon's water—locked away in rocks under the
surface—equals "about two and a half times the volume of
the great lakes."

—*The Week*, July 2-9, 2010

What other things, what other conditions, are locked away
improbably in rock—in an inhuman hardness?
Moses . . . doesn't the story go he smote
a rock in the wilderness with his staff and, lo,
therefrom the waters poured? And Mrs. Sommerson,
the Great Stone Face my mother called her,
regent of the Eighth-Grade Algebra Kingdom, she
who pity's violin strings couldn't move a quarter inch
from her unyielding scowl and decimal-pointed grade book . . .
when one evening I was late in leaving,
and quietly making my passage
down those eerily untenanted halls, I saw
her home room door was opened just enough to show her
at her desk, in tears, her head held in her hands
with such an autonomous weight, she cradled it
as if trying to rock into comfort a terrorized infant.

 ⌇

On page 290 of *In Flagrante Collecto* (a lovely book
about the loveliness found in conserving the world's
rejectamenta) is the photograph of a cast-lead woman,
a gardener, 2 ½ inches high, from 1935. She wears
a painted yellow bonnet and tilts a reddish-orange
watering can to a bold round flower; the arc of water
is red and green (it takes on some of the flower's color)
and sculpted in fanned-out wales, to give it "life."
I think of this figure when I read about the lunar water

disguised as a solid . . . water—only it's lead: like
water—only it's moon rock. Gone in a flicker,
only—it's imperishable. Instantaneous—only of long duration.
This might even serve to symbolize
our bifurcated . . . what would we call it, "nature,"
"mind," "self," "soul"?—the way that dolphins sleep

with only half of their brains at a time. *Our cousins.*
Or the way it's the ocean—only we wanted to walk on land,
so made it blood. All one of course, to the basic idea
of "oxygen delivery system." A photograph

I have of dolphins leaping in a circle, around
a full moon's great reflection . . . that reflection: is it "rock"
or is it "water," is it "sea" or is it "satellite"?
All one of course.

◡

By now I've seen all of the Great Lakes, but
I grew up in Chicago, and the north shore of Lake Michigan
—so nearly oceanic in its moods
and susurrations—is the lub-dub beat
that tugs my own heart's answering
vascular voice. If *that's* the element our bodies
are 92% of, no wonder we rage, then calm,
grow saturnine and winsome by turns, opaque
and lucid by turns. The stories I have

from Foster Avenue Beach, through my child-
and young adulthood, touch upon every essential aspect
of our humanity . . . death is there, and in the parked cars
and the writhing blankets over in a rocky corner
sex is there . . . the wall of fish smell baking in the sun
attends to them both . . . but right now
it's a photograph of my mother

I want to consider, black and white, from when
she must have been only a third of *my* age now . . . before
my father entered her life, and adult hope
and disappointment. It looks like spring. She's wearing
a poplin blouse and (European war is in the news)
a pair of sailor-looking shorts . . . *my mother had good legs!*
Not much background shows, yet you can tell

she's just above the sand, in the grass, reclining
on her elbows but with something . . . *alert* in her eyes,
which are turned to the lake, and to the lake breeze
lifting her collar and making dark drapes
out of her shoulder-length hair, that seem to be parting
to show us the promise of full-fledged womanhood rising
into her face. She's waiting

to open, she's waiting to grow in the light
as if she were a flower, and Lake Michigan were watering her

with the water in air—as later, I'd like to imagine,
the earth flowed over her with the water in dust.

His Creatures

"[The meat] of animals that had been whipped to death
was more highly valued for centuries, in the belief that
pain and trauma enhanced taste."

—B. R. Myers, in "Fed Up" *(The Atlantic)*

Finally the police knocked at his apartment door
for something worse. But this was bad enough.
A squirrel had been hit by a car, its back snapped
and its legs crushed, yet it wasn't dead: it
spasmed still, on the center line. And he'd slipped it
onto a cardboard sheet and carried it home, this
precious find, was watching it now in a rapture
as those twitches seemed to fill the table with extra,
desperate life, and down the table legs into the floor,
and from there to the bare walls, like a gourmet electricity
that made this room the most ecstatically
quivering cell on the planet! Although there's also
khoz özeeri, the traditional way the Tuva
kill a sheep: first, an incision is made
in the sheep's hide; then the slaughterer
reaches through, as lightly as possible and as knowingly
as if led inside by a guide, and severs the necessary artery
with his fingertips, the animal
woozily drifting away "so peacefully that one must check
its eyes to see if it's dead." The Tuvan term
means "slaughter" *and* "kindness." Alright; and the wick
that flickers so tremulously in *our* bodies? And
the way the cancer couldn't claim its daily inch of ground
without the scouts and the tanks and the camp followers
of pain, pain, pain? Why can't the God
my mother believed in learn from the best
of his creatures? Why couldn't I find him
with his arm stained in the slick of my mother's last fluids,
having entered her ribcage just enough
so that his thumb and forefinger might, with a gentleness,
pinch out her flame?

The Stem

He can tell each goat, Amando says
with a casual pride, by its shit. And Sophie
redoing her entire closet of clothes, and then
her job, and then her friends, around the glory
of her implants: there's a story of money
and sharp recuperation pain
behind those high-set beauties that smacks
of the mythic. And Cynthia lacquering
and threading another catalpa pod
that's added to the room-size nervous system
of catalpa pods the art museum has purchased,
for its aura of persistence and wonder.
The Buddha and his numinous Eastern cohorts
(not to mention many a Western sage)
encourage us to turn from all attachment
to the world and its things, the world
and its syrups and ukeleles and humidors
and ticket stubs and fish-shaped bottles of wine,
but I can think of nothing happier than Leonardo

encamped in the mountains, near the long-abandoned
copper and silver mines, filling the mule's
basketwork panniers with those rocks
in their spectrum of liver-red and rust-red, that
contain in their centers, like cochleas in ears,
the tiny coiled shells we normally associate
with beaches . . . carefully tapping them out, and
losing himself in contemplation; later
he'll return to his workroom, there to toy
with his army of fantastically painted pig-bladder balloons;
and, later still, he'll be in the refectory
preparing his pigments, smashing the boiled hooves
in with the eel-scum and the rose petals in a rich puree;

and never once will his nails be clean
of the heavy, beckoning sediments of his passions.
I can think of nothing happier

except, perhaps, my father
layering sugar and blackberries, sugar and blackberries,
into the great glass jugs where this
would alchemize into the thick and sticky brandy
he was famous for in the neighborhood (and how
he treasured that modest acclaim!), my father
stroking the prayer-fringe of his *tallis,*
fixing snow chains to the Chevy's tires, taking
the mason jars of pennies down to the bank each month
like votive offerings . . . *all* of this, every atom of this,
and none of this

for any of us is enough to secure our permanence,
not the digital album of id-unleashed cavorting
at the Jerusalem destination wedding,
not the beetle decorated with rhinestones
that the girl keeps pinned to a chain on her sweater,
not the slip-on circumcision cap
or the tasseled pasties or the mussels in butter,
none of it will keep us rooted here
beyond leave-taking, which is why,
at my father's death, when the stem

of connection to this world
was snapped, a few of us could hear, if just
for a second, the releasing scream, the cry
of violent displacement, as the body was forced at last
to let go of its avarice. It must be this
unbonding that the desert mystics
and tabernacle pulpit-thumpers warn us of,
this difficult secession—although
the difficulty itself must be one version of an eloquence
addressing the pleasures
of being here with my father's brandy
sweetening the tongue. And isn't that
what the tongue *is?*—one more stem

for the fullness. Cynthia licking
a last-minute sheen on another catalpa pod.
I can't guess how many deeply sexual
licks have heightened Sophie to another level.
One afternoon, in a light so much
like cream it could only have been in the south of France,
I saw Amando flick his tongue-tip
to a dried-out grass-inflected cake of scat:
"Lucinda's."

The Disappearance of the Nature Poem into the Nature Poem

There's my father, dead but standing
cheerfully on the horizon, in his skivvies
and his paintdrip-Pollacked "weekend pants,"
with all of his token appurtenances in piles
around him as surely as Tut was entombed and awoke
with small gold gods and small gold models of weaponry:
there's Duke's leash (Duke himself, he says, is
"right here": pointing over the horizon), and the jar of "chlorazine"
(some homemade suspension of cooling, antibacterial potency
he'd magic into existence every summer to quiet Frank Lamecka's rashy neck),
and the gallon of homemade cherry brandy he and my mother
toasted with (she's "right here," and he points again to what's obviously
a community just beyond my vision, auntie Hannah, uncle Lou,
the Dishkins from across the street . . .). Two or three times
a year, he does this. "Don't plotz, spondoolix,
I'm really here!"—yes: how can someone whose speech is as packed
as a mortadella *not* be there? "Don't dillydally,
shmendrick!" Every time, I walk over to meet him.
Every time, my first step closer finds him farther away
by exactly that step. It *is* the horizon, after all;

I've witnessed that come-hither prestidigitorial trick
ten thousand times. An afterlife—*is* there an afterlife:
my friends won't tire of arguing and their naked breaths,
coutured-up in the haze of a joint or a silky lilt of tea steam, swarm
to that unreachable place, and its unquenchable thirsts
and it unfindable Ali Baban, Eldoradon treasure hordes. Can "something"
come from "nothing"? What about "string theory"? And "God"? And why
the hell do women "etc. etc."? One step closer = just
as far apart: the Never Dance, that never halts,
its music is acoustically played on systole and diastole, its
electrical version is played across a synapse. And M? . . . today
she leaves for Houston, maybe *there* the nimble oncology docs,
those masterminds of burning and resplicing
our corporeal betrayals, will return the smile and poems

and gangly grace that have for a month now been distracted away.
"Maybe." *That's* the word on its gingerly way
toward the horizon. The tube up her nose and down the esophagus
is the rough shape of a question mark; it comes to stand
for everyone's concerns. But so far "question" inches up . . .
and "answer" keeps the inches-space between them steady. It's like

the disappearance—or what we thought would be the disappearance—
of the nature poem, "My heart leaps up when I behold a rainbow
in the sky," "The red-breast whistles from a garden-croft,"
the thrushes, larks and starlings . . . how could they survive
the 20th- and 21st-century city!—Kenneth Koch declares he wants
the particular smell of the Cincinnati fun park roller coaster
permeating a poem. And yet they do survive,
more meaningful than ever, perhaps, now that they're embattled,
dwindling, and fierce. And it depends on the definition
of "nature": now we've observed enormous geysers of water vapor
on one of Saturn's moons; now we can all be sharp Amerigo
Vespuccis of our glucose, of our DNA, our peptides
and our melatonin and myelin sheaths and neurons.
Like the horizon, "nature poem" forwards itself by increments
enough to remain inviolable—mysterious.
I've seen the starlings fly like a thread through a needle,
down into neutrinos and parsecs. There they are,
in the atomic charge in the chemicals in the cells in the blood
in my father's self-attacking heart. There they are, as someone cuts an opening
into M's dear body: a beating of wings and music.

Keats's Phrase

My father's been dead for thirty years
but when he appears behind my shoulder
offering advice, or condemnation, or a quiet pride
in something I've done that isn't even thistledown
or tiny shavings of balsa wood in the eyes of the world
—"Albie, grip in the middle and turn
with a steady pressure"—it's measurable,
if not the way the wind is in a sock,
or ohms, or net-and-gross, it registers the way
an absence sometimes does, and I listen to him
with a care I never exhibited when he was a presence,
alive, in his undershirt, chewing his tiny licorice pellets
and radiating a rough-hewn love. "Negative
capability"—the phrase of course is Keats's,

from his letters, but we make it ours a hundred times
a day. A hundred times we do our own pedestrian
version of early maritime cartography: the known world
stops, and over its edge the fuddled mapmaker writes
Here There Be Monsters and then illustrates
their non-existing coiled lengths and hell-breath
with a color-splotched vivacity he wouldn't waste
on inhabited shores. Or: "Don't think
of a polar bear!" . . . the game one plays
with a child. But I say with adult certainty that
when Eddie's wife Fiona went back to stripping
he couldn't stand to be at the club and see, and yet
those empty hours in his mind were populated just
as unbearably—and indeed, yes, there

were monsters in that void, and the vigilant bears
of insecurity and jealousy padded hungrily behind
his eyes each night until her return. For Keats,
however, the force that emptiness makes kinetic is
a positive one, the way that the invisible, unknowable
"dark energy" is seminal, a kind of funding agency
or sugar daddy powering the universe in all
its spangled beauty and veiled mystery
from behind the scenes. Last night, a woozy few of us
were mourning the demise of The Dusty Bookshelf.
"Well I *tried* to support it," I said, "by stopping in from time
to time." And B, the king of local kleptobibliomania, with
his nimble touch and expando-capacious overalls, said
"I tried to support it by *not* going in."

Smith's Cloud

It was like my father's religion
versus my teenage beatnik poetry
—his anvil-heavy leather-bound Old Testament
and my ratty paperback Ginsberg *Howl*
could argue, stamp their adamant textual feet all night,
could eat their way like bookworms through each other,
and yet neither would emerge from the collision
altered by even one word. Mostly, my childhood memories
are benign; we were short on money and long on affection.
My mother, although she made a show of reluctance,
still served separate food
to match the willful and disparate palates of my sister and myself;
she took us by the hand to the dime store,
to the library, where I signed up for my own card "like a major!"
Aunt Hannah repeatedly told the neighbors I had
"bedroom eyes"—whatever that was; at five or six
I only knew she thought I was the center of existence:
when I recognized a Pontiac or a Buick by its styling
she would coo as if I'd just translated Etruscan.
No one lied to me. Their promises were little but
were kept. Every winter my father got out the chains
for the tires. Every spring he fermented his sticky
homemade brandy, offering up this finished thing
to the world like a million-dollar jewel
on the balsawood tray I clumsied together in wood-shop class.
A kindness, even an innocence, was the dominant tone.
When Jimmy Semkins showed me he could pack
the usual snowball around a stone
for extra hurting power, it struck me
like news from some darker, alternate universe
—that understanding, and everything it implied,
hurt worse than the stone could. And in fact,
of course, my childhood *was* unknowingly congruent
with those other realms, more common perhaps
than mine, in which the twins are glittered-up to be pixies

and passed around the jerking circle like party favors;
in which the evening's food is what
you fight for, against the shanty rats;
in which you breathe when the iron law
of the iron lung allows you to breathe. . . . I think
of Smith's Cloud, the galaxy that's been, and is
even now, in the process of sailing through ours
(and us, through it) although it remains invisible and,
to me and to you in our daily go-round,
unregistered . . . an estimated mass of a *million* suns,
unfelt . . . it surely reminds us of Andy
and Angela: just three weeks out of their marriage
of seven years, and bumping into either one
we'd *never* guess they *ever* knew each other, somehow
nothing changed, his idiot grin,
her naughty-child pout . . . I saw her shopping yesterday,
in the strip mall lot she lifted her hands to the light
in a faux-excited greeting, and through her
and through me and really through you,
and the page, and the tree, and the wall, and the firmament,
neutrinos passed, and are passing now, a stream so steady
they didn't "pass" in a "stream" so much as be a sheet
unrecognized in us, a sheet of otherworldy substance,
as it passed through my aunt Hannah and through
the cousins of hers who were fed to the ovens of Dachau,
and through the best minds of my generation
I saw destroyed by madness, starving hysterical naked,
Sh'ma Yisroel, Adonai Eloheinu, Adonai E'chad.

Snow and Air and Irving

As much as some people want to believe there was only one Ralph [the swimming pig at Aquarena Springs in San Marcos, Texas], it's just not true: more than 700 pigs performed through the years. . . .

—Camille Wheeler, *Texas Co-op Power* magazine

The chanted oral history of the generations of Turtle People
is 80 recountable matrilineal turtle shells,
like stepping-stones, into the clan's past. . . .
Of the Mountain Ones, their lineage is recitable
through over 100 extended-family caves, the farthest back
in time as credibly real (by virtue of fetish-animal insignia)
as the nearest. . . .

∽

Jeanine said her father had wanted to be
a *National Geographic* photographer. Couldn't,
didn't, live that dream—but finally
earned his living working the giant four-color presses
where, among many other major periodicals,
National Geographic was printed. It struck me

how I couldn't say at all what my father's childhood
vision of future self was: fireman, rabbi, poker hustler,
tropical forest explorer—certainly not a guy
who daily peddled life insurance policies, which
is what he did become—and this is a pang,

a canine tooth, an incandescent canine tooth
in the heart, that gnaws away at night,
powered by frustration at how little I know of anything
preceding my own umbilical cord.

∽

But isn't there something essentially human in liberating
the present-moment me from the gravity drag
in the tunnel of blend-together ancestral anonymity!
(One thinks of that consciousness-moment in Western history
when artists start to separate themselves
from rote production, and sign their work, and cultivate
individual "styles.")
                    "Hello, my name is Catherine Selzberg-Wu,
I've made an inexpensive, but 'immeasurably moving' film
(that's quoted from the *Sacramento Star*) of cattle egrets
on the backs of one large herd, and as I speed and slow
and undulate the tracking of my camera, they appear
to be a line of italic printing, white
against the afternoon sky and a roseate plum
as the sun descends."
                    "Hello, my name is Intaglio Schwartz,
and this is true, a ship in the shape of a gondola
—green; a pea pod of an otherwordly ship—appeared
in the skies, and I was under it in the meadow
on that August day and was grazed by the light
it shone, and this is the only explanation I know
for why that very shape is now burned on my chest,
as you can see if you visit or see in the many
weekly picture magazines that made me a seven-day wonder,
admired and feared and jeered at and X-rayed
and shoved through a gauntlet of Geiger counters."

All of us: individual styles.

෴

I'm reading: "sixteen mummified Maori warrior heads
that have been on display in French museums
for more than a century" are going to be repatriated
"for burial in New Zealand," and a power is there
in those eerie spheres, most certainly a power, but
a blankness too, an interchangeable zeroness. So
today
I'm humbled more visibly in front of my friend Danelle,
whose courage is fighting to get her children back
from the Social Services system; and my friend Don,
whose contrition is his divorce, and whose divorce is a hook
in his brain that tugs its deepest catfish darkness;
and my friend Yvonne, whose pride is her collection
of 1950s doo-wop concert posters. . . .
"Hello,
my name is Albert Goldbarth, I'm trying to write
a poem, right now!"

And in the poem, successful or not, my father
is charged—by language and its fancies—
with immediacy, as if he were here,
alive, with my friends. He's fourteen, leaning awkwardly
(he means it to be cool) against the pool hall wall:
its beet-red brick has stored the sun all morning and now,
late afternoon, it enters with an intimate warmth
through his shoulders. He's watching the sixteen-year-old
woman-girls as they leave Green Pockets
—all of Chicago's lookee-lookee, rinky-tinky
energy in their hips—and enter a waiting limo
for who-knows-where. The May sun is a gilding
on their cashmered breasts, and one of the girls
allows her chest to brush against the chauffeur's hand
as he opens the door and she cat-slinks in . . . and then,

the perfect-polished vehicle giving off licks of sun like a torch,
they vroom away, and leave my father wishing
that he wants to be . . . when he "grows up" he wants to be
. . . a limo driver! *(Irv, you can do better than that.)*
A pool shark! *(Irv . . . the sun, remember the sun?)*
An astronomer! *(Yes! Not that it will come to this.)*
"Hey, Irv!"—his friend, Jeanine's father, crosses the street.
"See? See? I got it!" With the money he saved last winter
shoveling snow, he's purchased a Kodak Brownie camera,
his life's first camera . . . and his hands shake as he aims
and makes my father his first portrait.

⌒

Where does the shoveled snow go? Ice.
Or slush; and then water. And then the air.
It's all one to the gods. One element
in its various masks. I suppose to the gods
the elements, even, are masks
—of particle fields. Planets come,
ho-hum, and planets go. . . .

A poem is frozen language,
as language is thought we've fixed
in speech or in a dictionary,
as thought is neuroelectrical force
with a boundary . . . all of it

snow to the gods,
water to the gods, or air; they've seen it all,
the Turtle girls now 80 generations back
no different than Angel and Annalisa
slinking out of a limo and fucking around
in a party house with gangsta guys who self-morph
in and out of Maori warriors. . . .

So, yes, if we shout a little too egocentrically loud,
it's only because we fear—but must admit
the cosmic majesty of—the gods' aloof regard
as my father locks a lid on his childhood dreams
and enters the dun-brown offices of the Metropolitan Life Insurance Company
to apply for a job, and is
[in units of Ralph the swimming pig] one body

swimming through the karma of 700 bodies.

Song

One essential difference between the sun and the wheat
is that when the light's as finely milled
as possible in falling through the gears of leaves
—tossed, and parsed, and exquisitely ground in use—
it lands at last on the Earth as complete
as it ever was; *not dead, not dead yet,* sings
some hidden bird in a richly verdant
pompadour of a bough, whose job is evidently overseeing
light and leaves and providing appropriate commentary.
Even the wheat, I suppose we could say, is *changed*
by the thresher, and then the mill, but dead
to only those who have never seen the soul
steam out of a freshly opened loaf at The Bread Lady's
up the street, or stood in front
of heraldically at-attention stalks that someone over
4,000 years ago painted on the side of a tomb exactly to be
a symbol of resurrection . . . *I've been here every spring
forever,* says the bird, and in the bounds of a certain logic
that's inarguable. Millennia of ancient Egypt, wheat
and golden scorpions and Jews and war and cosmetic palettes,
have been made less than chaff now in the gnashing teeth
of time, but see the lines of thousands a day
at the museum exhibit or follow the bitter international
lobbing of invective over repatriation!—the pharaohs
are alive as ever. I'm thinking of
my mother, holding a bolus of dough, the cigarette that certainly
will kill her (in the bounds of a certain symbology,
it's inarguable) set down and unattended
in a plastic dimestore ashtray for the moment,
and its length of ash is a measurement of her absorption in
(and befuddlement over) the arcane advice of a recipe pamphlet
handed out for free by Richland Flour Company: how
alive she is!—how full of calories buzzing about in puzzled thought,
her mind in a puddle of spooned-out butter and discouragement
and aimless tuneful humming. Or I *want to be* thinking

of that, it's so "poetic," but in fact I'm merely remembering
telling a friend that a journal's accepted seven new poems of mine
and she says back *Well you aren't* and no, I'm not,
unless I am by the time you read this, *if* you read this,
if there's "time" outside of human awareness, sixty-seven
this year, a cairn of light the light creates of itself
on the front porch planter, *not dead yet,* and the bird flies off,
maybe to your house, to sing its amazing message there.

EVERYDAY
LIFE ON
PLANET
ALBERT

Secondary

En route to the Earth—that's
the pure part, that's when the light
of the Sun is uncontaminated
and in its richest glory. And then

it arrives here, and it necessarily
dwindles and thins: becomes that leaf,
this lake, the dazzle off cars in traffic,
my wife asleep in the sheets.

Dickens points out that water in which
the goldsmiths washed their hands was sold
to refiners, having a secondary,
yet still impressive, value.

Noon

The shadow completely
reenters its barn.

Jung / Malena / Darwin

A man could stumble into the consulting room
with werewolf all around him. A woman
would swear she flew. Another, spectral meetings
with emissaries from outer space. It isn't surprising
Jung believed that everyone bears
a "shadow self," an extraextensional
him or her; nor should it be surprising
I believe *him,* I agree: another
possibility-field is furled inside us and,
at some chance cue, will opportunistically
open. Only that explains where N goes to,
when W's asleep. Tomayto /

tomahto. Malena is synesthesiac; "o"
is black for her, so "orange" isn't really
orange—her two incompatible hers
in sibling rivalry. Orange reminds me:
Florida. Amazingly enough, in 2003
the aurora borealis was visible
as the water-skiers stopped inscribing their esses over the water
and the orange pickers halted in a grove,
with an almost religious glaze to their eyes,
as somebody else's sky grew superimposed
on theirs. When N drags home in the wee hours,
W's still asleep: and dreaming of L. When Darwin

thought to test sonic responses of earthworms,
he requested that his children serenade
his soily jars of them: and, dutifully, an orchestra
of whistle, bassoon, and piano began
concatenating the night away in the billiards room,
its air alive with tremble and skreek,
lowblown moan and high-pitched tootle, so
racketing you'd think the row of dead wrens
and the barnacles might rise up and start capering.
The worms appeared deaf to that music; nor,
I'll bet, does this concert sound like a day
in *your* world—though it's *of* your world.

Deep Ink

It's not just that grief is a glutton, but
an omnivore. *Anything*
she offered, it took—her art; her sex;
her daughter's christening. . . . When those
ran out, it fed directly

on her. It made her own subconscious
traitorous: *come bivouac here; and eat;*
and eat. We could see . . . see
her shoulder bones emerging like a sentence's
stark diagram, from out of luscious prose.
We could see it the way they saw
grief bend with hunger over the streets of Paris

in 1870, four long months into Germany's siege
of that city: the lines would form at four a.m.
for a miserly portion of horses' hooves. The front edge
of a breath on Christmas Day would freeze before
the back edge exited, and meals were made
of mules, sparrows, crows; most former rat-catchers
reinvented themselves as butchers, and the government

slaughtered the animals in its state zoo: camel,
reindeer, yak, the porcupines, the bears, two elephants
children knew by name. It's a pity
the Louvre had been converted (with sandbags covering its windows)
to government headquarters. What some artist
could have made, in painting this horrible
two-tier system! . . . a woman in rags, bent holding a cat
with both hands, slobbering, relishing it,
just as—shown very spectrally, but credibly—grief bends

its mouth to her. And some of us understand,
or think we understand, such overwhelming woe, although
we haven't experienced it. We think we've been inoculated;
spared it, through a tease of it
—in the way of the dinner I ordered,

out with friends: black pasta,
ribbons of black, black pasta,
colored by squid ink.
What does it taste like! What does it taste like!

Not a flavor, so much;
an intimation.

Big Things

The name "crocodile" comes from *kroke* (pebble) and *drilos* (lizard), an
example of the Greek habit of using diminutive language for something
grand: Cf. "pyramids" = "wheat cakes."

—John M. Marincola

I maintain the Greek word *doesn't* reference the smallness
of the pebble, but the pebbled look of a crocodile's hide.

Still, the idea is inescapable: the interplay
of sizes. When particle physicist Murray Gell-Mann theorized

hadrons (that is, protons and neutrons) were made up
of even smaller particles, Richard Feynman suggested

naming them partons, after Dolly's 40DD
humdingers. Sizes: the apple tree, complete in thought already,

inside the pip. The way the mote from space is complicit,
every year, in 30,000 metric tons of "space dust"

tumbling onto the Earth. The epic poem of the human egg
and the journeying sperm (that's 85,000 times smaller)

has yet to find its Homer—unless we're all, both
women and men, a group Homer. The way

a crazed and driven 19th-century cetologist is entering
the partially hollowed-out body of a blue whale

with his lantern, like a miner into a cavern
("some of its blood vessels are so wide that you

could swim down them"—David Attenborough), while someone
else is measuring the whorls of the Polynesian land snail

Partula down to eight decimal points . . . their fascinations
are equal. Sizes: which is larger, a scruple

or a transgression? How the one struck ivory key
completely fills Symphony Hall. Sizes: the Neanderthals, those losers

in the evolution sweepstakes, none the less had brains
"significantly larger than those of modern people"

by up to four-tenths of a liter. The way
the model is the height of the painter's thumb.

In the eighth grade it was commonly known that "Saucy" Chenowitz
—and she did everything within the powers of décolletage

to foster this assessment of her burgeoning—had "pyramids,"
while Clare Ledoux, in the metaphorical system

we inherited, was "as flat as a pancake." This implied
a hierarchy in which "poor Clare" was relegated

in mammary units to peon and, as I remember, scorn
and pity attached to her . . . although I also remember that

when four of the muscle-knotted oafs we called "the Fuckhead
Five" began to beat up on Lydia Roosevelt because

she *was* Lydia Roosevelt—our first and only Negro, bussed
for an hour every day from south of downtown—and Lydia's

skin broke open, blood and dust in an ugly uneasy
twill across the ground, a few of us—Saucy included—

scooted away in shock, and the rest of us stood there
as dumb as cattle in shock, and Clare Ledoux

leaped into that tangle whirling her fists . . .
fear, and courage, and sheer bullheaded decency

thumping inside her breast.

Our Reference

Sometimes we need to see it
in a different way of seeing it

—the laundry, the boringly everyday laundry
flapping on a line to dry

is seraphic, and slightly whimsical,
in the photo of someone's everyday laundry

flapping on a line to dry.
And the everyday love

is cubist after all-night drinking.
God's grace is a picture frame

we place around our disappointed hopes.
He's mysterious, God is. Then again, so is

the squid as it runs through the range of its skintone colors
the way a pianist does the scales. And

an Amazonian tree frog in the frame of the *National Geographic*
photo is almost a pastry, almost cloisonné in its glazing, but

I wouldn't suggest you lick its toxic body. It
makes "green," that we've known all our lives,

into something outside of our reference. A peignoir
on the clothesline: third-world garment factory hell?

or sexy allure? The breeze uplifts, by an inch of implication,
its seafoam peekaboo hem.

If you wet a towel, then twist it hard and tight
to beat your child,

it isn't laundry anymore.

To This

My friend X, who was sleeping with Y, who wanted Z,
who was sleeping with no one but dreaming the hairs

and uric tang and heavenly tremolo voice of A. . . .
This never halts; if it's folded back in us like yolk

into dough, invisibly, the way it is in the nun
or priest, it never halts, it drives us to distraction

and to progeny, to sonnets and to crack cocaine,
it ticks—this species need to meld

and variegate and increase—in the smallest
titrate portion of us forever. Even when the flying saucers

strike one night against our planet in the movie,
and those huge "atomic ray" explosions fill our vision—even

then, the plot includes—the plot very forcibly
makes room for—the woman and the man

in their dramatic pas de deux of exultation and jeopardy,
effort and swoon and defeat

so far removed from the concerns of outer space invasion.
Thus it was that Nikki and Benjamin exited

the movie theater, and underneath the discussion
of rocket launcher special effects, they were covertly

loving each other and hating each other
and half-infatuated over someone else, out loud

and unstoppably. The Martians desire dominion
over all the Earth. But then so do the genes,

that have brought us to this.

"An isosceles triangle
was the same on Earth or Mars."
—Henry Kuttner

Millennia later, tendriled archaeologists from another galaxy
land on Earth—an arid, pitted place but with
the skeletons of some early race of bipeds. One
configuration is common; it was there on Mars as well,
and on the planet of genius leeches in their murky broth,
and the planet of sentient airborne puffs,
and the planet of living metal. Two of the skeletons
are buried (here they "buried" the dead) together,
side by side, with the arm bones touching as if
there existed an intimacy that lasted into the grave.
And yet one cranium is turned to face a skeleton buried
yards away: "the longing" is how they describe it in their notes.
They have found this triangle on every world they've visited.

Oh

How near would we have to be
(in its blood? in a sex-grip with it?)
and how exactly congruent with the circadian speed
of its life span,

                    for the massive clattering ratchet
of the mechanisms of flight—the wings,
the calibrating tensile links—to sound
on an appropriate scale, instead of blended
into *our* perception of the thin,
annoying whine of the mosquito. . . .

ᔐ

And conversely . . . when the beams we've packed so tightly
with a summary of what we've learned *(we know pi!*
and Fibonacci spirals!) as well as the beams
of our entertainments and news
at last reconstitute themselves in the receptors
of a planet so galactically removed from us
that our definitions of "light" and "time" no longer count . . . what
trivial spritzle of gibberish will they hear
in what we once knew as the porn star's
nearly carnivorous moan of pleasure
or the moan of the dying six-year-old
who was out in the desert playing with her invisible friends
when the tanks appeared?

ᔐ

Once in wooing a woman, and
in trusting her discernments, I discovered
—independent of my volition, is how it felt—
our bar booth had turned to a confessional: and from out
of the coal pit in me; out of the acrid, boggy
cavity where the fossils are stored; from deep
in the collider tunnels where I was engaged in a physics game
of tag-you're-"it" with "black holes" and "god particles";
and rising on a trellis of wish, a gantry of animal snarl;
with the superstructure of armies in collision and yet
with the careful finesse that wouldn't jostle a single mouthful
of matzoh toppings . . . a story came forth
of everything I believed in, and suffered, everything
that made my dormant adrenaline uphackled
in its chemical version of quills, and expectantly ready
for an amazing journey . . . *everything,*
which *she* heard as the distant, tiny humming
a superior species would shoo away with a flick.

⁓

The Greeks. The Romans. Mostly, though,
thegreekstheromans . . . mingled back there
somewhere in a layer of antiquity paste.
Their myths exist to remind us
stars and dust are individuals
who grieved, and exalted, and pondered
stars and dust, and then became them.

A woman who was alive when Plato was alive
gave birth; or came; or kneeled senseless at the graveside
with the same unplumbed profundity of moaning
as a woman just this afternoon . . .although
we have no stethoscope to set against
the dust—or the stars—to bring that
eloquent breath back into a living articulation.

A mountain is *here*. A mountain is *so* here,
and it isn't going anywhere. We're the lace hem
of a mountain, a kind of delicate doily surrounding its base
with beauty worked into us only because
of the empty holes that lace requires.
Thousands of mouths. *Billions* of mouths.
Not that the mountain cares about the oh
and ah, ohh and ahh, ohhh
and ahhh and ohhhh and ahhhh.

Ong / Eugene / Monet

I am from Singapore and I am experiencing a mysterious
phenomenon. My neighbor living downstairs have radiation all
over his body. The radiation can extend as far away as the Moon.
He is able to use this to go inside my body and manipulate my
body parts. He can do this over incredible distances even when I
am overseas. Please reply soon. Ong Hock Ching.

—excerpted from an email to *Fortean Times*

Okay, so we can all agree that Mr. Ching is
seriously woowoo. Then again, I've read
string theory and dark matter and Higgs boson,
and no matter *where* we draw the line it seems
its other side is always farther off than sanity
allows. Today in walking up a trail

through a standard Kansas field—wheat,
as high as my shoulder, rustling
unidirectionally in the breeze—I'm struck
by how I'm walking over what was once
an ocean bottom, how its slitherlife
the size of oil pipelines swam and coupled here . . .

and how if I could touch the Moon
I'd touch the Earth—the part gouged
cataclysmically out of its side.
My friend Jeanine would often visit Eugene,
the zoo's black rhino, stand still, beam
her thoughts his way—his heavy, plated

way—until he'd nose up to the fence
and she could stroke his horn: it must have been
like reaching through a unicorn, to touch
the true, hard thing inside the fiction.
We think that after his cataract surgery Monet
saw ultraviolet: he could see the everyday radiance

outside of our limited range.

215 N. Fountain

We figure it's fifty miles of sex—of floral sex—
between the birds' enthusiastic gulping
of those beckoning red berries, and their shitting

the seeds to the grass below our front yard tree.
Another invisible system attaching 215 N. Fountain
to the world. Some nights on our porch it's easy

to scan the sky, its esplanade of stars
against the nothing, and believe this house is something
that the solar system's gloried-and-catastrophied its way toward

since its first discrete emergence from what Robert Chambers
called, in 1844, the "fire-mist." Well, some attempts
to place the Earth and the sky in a logical, patterned cahoots

are rubbish: Pliny was wrong, suggesting excavated
prehistoric axes are "petrified thunderbolts." Still,
for his far age, this passes as a best guess, and we see how attractive

it must have been, to draw that causal line from "then"
to "now." I remember the days when it seemed
the-woman-who'd-become-my-wife and I first met on an atom

of time that was, as in a diagram, preceded and led into
by a force in the shape of a riverine or arboreal branching
going back before the first transition fish

dreamed legs. A thousand generations of DNA
and traffic flow and weather maps and pilgrim routes
predestined our initial night of sweet and fumbling love

—or so it felt to us. It's "magical
thinking" . . . the kind that says since two men named Doug Finnegan
("total strangers to each other") wrecked their indentical '09 Subarus

head-on at Main and Kirkendell, the universe itself
was born, was teeming with plankton
and refugee camps and diamond-stud designer bras,

for just that pinpoint cymbals-smash. It isn't magic,
though—just labor (and humbling in its expertise) when
someone charts the travel of a pathogen through three streams

in the uplands and through two different species
inhabiting those streams, to explain—and hopefully cure—
its first malicious flowering in a five-year-old

in New Delhi. Look: so pretty, that chart, so almost angelic
a feather! And so I'm back to birds. Today
my wife is gardening. By "today" I mean

"the accumulated entirety of yesterdays." *Everything.*
Everything has come to this. And empty
or profound (as the mood of the moment decrees), that

can't be denied. She waves to me; the Stone Age,
then the Bronze, and then the Iron,
Plastic, E-Chip, have deposited us here,

in our skins, in the moment.
Already she's idly scratching away
at the poison ivy the birds transported.

The Point at Which My Wife Enters a Poem about the *National Geographic* Cover Story (November 2009) "Are We Alone?"

—by which it *doesn't* mean in the bedroom or dining room,
but the universe. The answer is a demi-hopeful
"possibly not," although whatever other life exists
Out There in the petit point billions of planet possibilities might be
no more than a gelid smear that quivers in light
and quiets in the darkness, or a philosophically minded gas.
We've come far, from the need to see our Terran selves
as singular—as "God's elect" and central in His cosmos—
to a people simply hungry for companionship and, naturally, curious
about our neighbors . . . even if by neighbors I mean
theoretical beings twenty light-years off in space. That's
the distance of Gliese 581d and Gliese 581e: is *that* where life is,
liquid and almost-familiar? Something swimming with electrical vim
and means of reproduction in an alien
but no-so-alien H_2O? The planet with atmosphere
trailing behind it cometlike, a bridal gown with the train on fire. . . .
The planet with acetylene lakes. . . .
The planet entirely surfaced-over by ever melting rock. . . .
Is there life on Fomalhaut 6?—is *that* where life is,
viral, spiral, flippering over in salty waves, not unlike
the elephant seal on page 76 of this same issue,
who stares at the *National Geographic* camera
with his own biocular sense of the world, his own
mammalian alien-but-not-so-alien consciousness. . . . Page 95
begins a series of striking full-page portraits
of the Hadza, a Tasmanian hunter-gatherer tribe
whose Earth both is and isn't mine. . . . "A hunting knife
is strapped to his hip, in a sheath of dik-dik hide. . . .
He can converse with a honeyguide bird
(they whistle back and forth) and so is led directly
to a teeming beehive. . . . He sits cross-legged at his fire
and eats the baboon's cheeks, the eyeballs,
the neck meat, the forehead skin. . . . The men

tell campfire stories, the women sing. . . ." And this
is the point at which my wife enters the poem
from a day of teaching and then a quickie stop at Town East Mall,
her body the same percentage of periodic-table elements as mine,
and her invisible halo of oxygen-carbon-in-and-out-accordion-squeeze
a thriving aura of colleagues and students
and stoplights and Twitters and crazyass dreams
I understand and I don't understand, and at night
(the man is typing, the woman is singing in her bath)
I want companionship *so* much, if it's there, if I can find it
orbiting me in bed, if I can see it . . .
I *think* I see it . . . and then it's eclipsed for one dark moment;
now it's here again; and now it dims and ducks and slips away. . . .
But then, "planet" *means* "wanderer."

Wings

The high-school-level soccer game,
Nathan and Holly cheering Aidan's efforts
in their inevitable singularity pose: he's
on the bleacher seat, she's snuggled
between his open knees, as mingled-up
as a centaur. On the field
of fourteen-year-olds' honor, Troy smacks into Ithaka
with an echo of the ferocity
remaining from the Big Bang. None of the ancient stories
disappears; they only slip into
their gangsta and catwalk and NASCAR attire.
What's the annihilation-clash of matter and antimatter
if not a succubus and an incubus
going at each other?

୬

Is this your neighborhood? I'm guessing
yes, and in any case you recognize this lawn
in green with the tricycle in cardinal red
left on it, like the junior version of H. G. Wells's
Martian war machines. The rainbow-tailed
windsocks on the porch. Smiley welcome mats.
We never hear it directly, but our inner
psychic stethoscope is picking up the *shrik*
of swords being slid from their scabbards; and tiny fires
sizzling in their braziers on the altar-tops;
and the garlanded bull, the unblemished one,
being led by the priests from its cavern.
The wingéd gods descend with the sound
of awnings in a brisk wind.

The Song of Us against Vaster Patterns

At first her nipples are featureless, and he thinks
of those statues he's seen in the Middle East
that many centuries of men's hands
have rubbed smooth, for luck. Later,
as their afternoon dalliance enters
second gear, she proudly and wordlessly points
to them—they're richly corrugated now—
and then points to the two, tight, dusk-pink roses
that he'd brought and placed together
in a glass vase on the bedside table . . .
yes, the kinship is obvious.

The lung; and the sea.
The heart; and the mysterious pulsing
of radiation in nebulae light-years distant.

⁓

Is it comforting, to set the cursive script
written over our brains against the burning
spiral lobes of Van Gogh's sky, then set
his paintiverse against the actual petaled wheel
of stars we call the galaxy?—yes, comforting,

consoling even, to sense the replication
of our lives in vaster patterns; as in waking first
and studying her shut lids while they flutter and
then open to conscious day, the way
Persephone or Inanna returns from the underworld's dark halls;
comforting . . .

or diminishing?—to see that
we're the universe's footnotes: "Oh yes,
here too, in these little peripheral lives."

～

"Ignorant armies clash by night," says Matthew Arnold
in "Dover Beach," the armies of ten-year-old African children
who think God makes them bulletproof, the armies
of drug cartels removing faces with X-acto knives
and leaving them on the families' stoops, the armies
of petro-nations shouting *oil oil oil* the way the frat boys shout
for pussy under sorority windows all night, my sister
the Civil War, my sister the Korean War, the Afghanistan War,
my sister a tiny engraving of the *Iliad,* all of its blades
and running blood, my sister a Cliffs Notes
for the story of the Trojan Horse, my sister
against a background of nations drawing
swords, spit-shining missile silos, the war
on drugs, the war on poverty, if there's a war
on cancer does it imply that cancer wages war
on us, my sister so little,
my sister her biopsy,
my sister with her fingers crossed,
my sister may the earth and the sky
convene at the horizon
and negotiate détente.

～

An open book, abandoned in a field.
When the wind blows to the left,
the pages blow to the left.
And, in the background, the same for the wheat.

Go Too

The fish is so large, and the tough, determined bird
with its claws hooked in is so small,

the bird looks like a surfer
on this northwoods lake. Meanwhile,

a moan from farther off—the greenery is thick,
but not enough to muffle this—sounds all

too human, although whether pleasure
or distress I can't determine without a visual.

Meanwhile, the war. Meanwhile, a violent geyser
of ammonia on one of Jupiter's moons, a hundred miles

tall. So much "meanwhile"! The marriage,
the drug cartel, the feathers daubed onto a cowrie-shell mask.

What can we do? What can we ever do
but "do" itself—exist,

in the brine and the duff and the flowering spume
of the moment. How Zen. How very Zen.

The planet takes a planet-breath and dives
the way a whale dives

magnificently through the universe, and the mites
on its skin go too.

Doozie

"A bun in her oven? Geeze Louise, that isn't
the malarkey? *Estelle?* Miss Goody-Two-Shoes?"
      "I thought it was bunkum too,
when I heard it. Really: you coulda knocked me
for a loop. But Alice told me, and she's jake."
Alice: the provenance, the gatekeeper. So it *wasn't* all hooey.
It was the real goods. Aunt Ruby
hadn't shown up for her visit last month and,
well, Estelle was in a pickle, was between the proverbial
rock and its cousin the hard place, friendless,
paddleless up that famous defecatory creek and down
in the dumps, and while vernacular studies

isn't my speed, I love the way we used to talk.
We also used to say the autumn light is lambent
on the lake top, and the waves display a heraldic curl
as in halcyon days . . . and that was also a fine,
fine thing to say. Or that some multibody hid
his second exoneural projecto-self in a pocket of subspace,
masking it over with molecules of landscape-sim
. . . that's how they talk in sci-fi-ville, while over
in the empirical records of science, someone is saying
the reagent deliquesces although
in its previous state it underwent resorption. All
of the languages are appropriate to their purposes—are

fine. Jack Gilbert's poem in honor of *wabi*
—that's the Japanese word for, roughly,
finding a beauty in ruin that one can *only*
find in ruin—reminds us that to lack the word
for a concept is really to lack the concept.
Let the word occur, though, and then suddenly
in a fingersnap, in a trice, and like a bolt out of the blue,
I can see my friend for whom Estelle is an avatar
in stanza one, and the formerly unacknowledged
stores of dignity and perseverance
that carried her through the shame of the abortion
—her *wabi*—flower forth. One story goes

she fucked up big-time, Mick was a saint but
nooo, she had to get knocked up by a douchebag
like Kenny. Another story: her mind is part disassociative, and
so requires positive reinforcement from multiple sources.
Actually they're the same story, only told in different languages.
Or actually because they're different languages, they're
different stories. In mine, she's just returned
from the doctor, and needs to tell Mick. She's sitting
surrounded by thousands of happy memories—the light
through the louvers is lambent—but we all know
how the story goes: life is jim dandy, a peacheroo, then
words get spoken, and overnight the whole world goes kablooey.

Away

Bad design: that 1940s oh-my-god
"Lone Ranger child's toothbrush": yes, the child

would need to put the muzzle inside his mouth.
A gun-shaped whistle, the same. Bad design:

a child's plastic water gun in the shape of a tiger:
the trigger is thoughtlessly placed

where the penis would normally be. A Donald Duck
and a dinosaur, the same. Bad design:

the male urinary tract going straight
through the prostate—so, when the latter enlarges

with age, the former is blocked to a terrible stutter.
I remember my urologist inserting an optical fiber

up the length of my penis, fiendishly hand-cranking it
every agonizing micro-scream of the way, until I thought

—the "fiendishly" may be overdoing it, but I did
think this—that dying would be the better

option. Henry Petroski's many books on engineering
provide a number of fascinating examples of bad design

from bridges to paper clips, but death is what I had in mind
this week—the too-white onslaught of the leukemia

that softened up my father for his heart's conclusive
sucker punch, and the delicate but hardening doily lace

the cancer worked throughout my mother's lungs,
for instance—and whatever Newtonian laws

or evolutionary biology or tales of an original Edenic
misstep wove this inevitability into our chromosomes,

I think it's a bad design, I'm thinking of Bob King
and of Peggy Rabb, of how they rode out of existence

so completely, we wept for them like little children.
Hi yo, silver. Away.

The Song of What We See

Of course the sun is "out in space."
It's "up." It's "away." However

at dawn, in its immanence,
we can believe that the light is generated

here, low set amid the stems
of the grasses, in a weakly saffron

leaking-out of the radiation
our science texts call "solar" but

seems formed in the heart of the Earth.
One more example of that perfect

trickster, perspective. The way
the painter's model across the room

is the height of the painter's thumb.
The way the proudly postured amplitude

of her breasts exerts a gravity
in his mind, all night, of greater

demanding force than does the body
of the woman who is actually and trustingly

asleep at his side, in contact. Or the way
the deeply—the neurally—storaged memory of the ardencies

of his youth can overpower the reality
of his middle age, betraying him

repeatedly into foolishness. And somewhere,
says the news, six hundred people have died

in an army attack in a country the name of which
is nearly gibberish—compare that

to the buzzsaw boil of flies that writhes
across the bloody face of a corpse in the field

you're walking through. We see
what we see. And therefore we must understand

and forgive those earlier ones—among them
our equals; some of them, our superiors—who

knew for a fact the sun circles the world.
And haven't I driven in joy

or panic (or sheer confusion between the two),
across the plains of Kansas, and stopped

my car at the roadside, and leaped on out
to collapse in a lightheaded sprawl

with the soil gripped in my fists and my face
to the sky, on the undeniably flat, flat Earth.

Benny

That night she had a dream: *she died,*
and on the marble mortuary slab she was gutted

and butterflied

into equal halves; and each
was an entire her.

And her sister had the same dream.

∽

They were identical twins, with the usual
naughty deployments and confusions:
fooling the frat boys in a dim-lit bedroom;
startling at the sudden
almost-me around a corner.

"Later, our lives took . . . different paths."
Who do you get when a sixth-grade science teacher is turned
completely inside-out?
She's waiting in room 7 for the john to show up
with the needles he promised.

Light in an experiment
will do it: divide
                    along two routes
                    and still be a single light.

We say "twins." But in the dream
there's only one woman

under two moons,
making two loves,

casting two shadows,
counting two pulses.

⌒

Palping all four breasts
for the lump.

⌒

And me, the man who's writing this?
I *wasn't* "on drugs,"
it *wasn't* "a religious vision," the night

I walked below the sky's own nervous system
of stars, in the tree-whisper dark, it was simply
the Truth of Things, the Way of It, that
I was suddenly hyperaware of my Other

out there somewhere . . . you have yours as well . . . who
paced the bottom-slag of the pit
when I was joyous, who was levitatingly joyous
when I was caged and lost
from any moral compass; and I saw

how, in the instant that the face of falling snow
looks into the face of the water,
there is, before it dissolves, a recognition

of reunion; how the cliffs of the east
and the beaches of the west still argue
across the time zones, over
which of them their mother the universe
loves better.

⌒

A moment/place existed when/where
Space and Time were in the same womb.
Dying here, as we all are,
on this Earth, at this speed, in this whirl of mortal abundance,
it's impossible to tell the two apart.

Words too: the twins in them.
Tear *(air)*. Tear *(ear)*.
Or niggah—it depends on who says it.
When I was ten I found this hilarious:
rubber balls and liquor.

༄

The sun is lowering
into the milo fields
and into the highway scissoring through them,
touching both,
the same.

One sister looking out the window
into the other cars, imagining she can recognize
the sharpies, the players, the lucky and rich
beelining into the city for some
uptempo rendezvous made of money and skin.

One sister studying a fence-hawk
as the deepening sunset fills it
like a jar with clover honey.

༄

When I woke, it was a flybuzz afernoon
in the market: my begging bowl
with the lovely spiderweb grain in the wood was empty.

When I woke, the view of downtown
from my penthouse atrium window was a puzzle
compounded of silver and glint.
When I woke, the balalaika.
When I woke, the campfire smoke like a python
curling around the tent.
When I woke, the bong; the call to mobilize on the ridge;
the catwalk model slipping her hundred-dollar spaghetti straps
off her thousand-dollar shoulders; the spiking line
on the cardiac patient's chart; the host
with Christ inside; the fortune cookie with a blandishment;
the chacha champion's trophy.
When I woke, I left my other life
for this one. When I slept, I returned.
When I woke, the revolution had flipflopped everything
I knew and believed in.
When I woke, the cradle.
When I woke, the whip; the rotisserie; the chakra.
When I woke, my eyelids fluttered
like two petals of an infinitely petaled flower.

Cognates.

೨

"One day they arrested her for soliciting.
By then the state was already set to take my sister's child.
But after the cancer spread to her lymph nodes
that was moot. And so Benny is mine now.
He's three. We're getting along, working it out.
He calls me what he always has:
he calls me 'Mommy Auntie.'"

Midnight

The ones who see the stars.

The ones who see the emptiness.

SELFISH

After the Broken Shoulder,

I thought of the force in the fish. I did
my exercises. I extended my ailing arm along the table
into the lipped, resistant cincture of the rosebud
of my pain, until it widened, until
I made it a sleeve of small glass stabs
I entered, up to the wrist, then higher,
moving into the pain, and thereby changing the pain,
as somewhere else the vapor altered itself
through multiplying itself and so returned
to Earth as rain, the poet of rhyme and rule
lay down beside the poet of crazy slam
and there was to-fro sexual spelunk
and neither one would write the same again, the force
was an immanence steeping
into a deeper-dyed idea of itself inside the fish,
was like the dream of the hand of a puppeteer
in a live and literal fish, I pushed
one quarter-inch of veldt and grassy plain and asphalt alleyway
at a time across the top of that impossible table, now
the fins were nearing a pebbled shelf, as somewhere else
the sugar inside of the twig was nearing green,
and the writhe in the web was a sugar closer to wings,
and the atoms of hand in the atoms of fin
were alchemizing, up to my elbow, higher,
wearing the pain, reducing the pain in wearing the pain
from here to its horizon line, my twenty reps, the grains of sand,
the first step and the first breath,
and I clambered out onto the land.

My Personal Mythology

From a list of weaknesses to weed out, in Jeffrey Levine's
instructional "On Making the Poetry Manuscript":
    [15] Proof for the Big Abstractions (i.e., "infinity,"
        "eternity")—the 19th century is over.
    [16] Proof for the small abstractions (i.e., "dark")—
        the 19th century is still over.

There came a time when enough of my friends were dead,
or dying, or vexed by trident-wielding imps

of neurological pain, that when I walked out
into the nighttime, I was less aware

of the soft—the almost velvety—crunch of gravel
underfoot, and the twelve beer bottle empties

someone had patterned into the look of a loose
but ritual circle (into a Glasshenge?) than I was

of the black, blank inches in between the stars
that translate—once they're properly rescaled—

to infinity, the boundlessness so far
beyond imagination—which, by definition, requires

images—that it's even beyond the language
of *attempting* to imagine. It's like this 1950s

British science fiction adventure magazine I won
at auction, the spiffy *Worlds of the Universe,* its cover art

a spaceship of the old-school, fish-finned,
light-years-devouring sort, with cast of valorous

spacefarers to match, the vérité detail (down
to every rivet, every glint on a fishbowl helmet) lending

a physical plausibility and immanence . . . but surely
the title implies there must be "worlds" that are *not*

"of the universe," too? Eternity? . . . are they "eternity"? . . .
is *this* where my friend Dottie finally went to

after months of gurgling a hushed diminuendo
into her hospice tubes, her eyes—because her tongue

was gone—requesting release, and silently
but eloquently saying she *knew* she was going somewhere

only a word like "glory" might start to indicate, and
she wouldn't be restrained by the bucket of chum

or the scatter of kibble or even the marble chips like foam
around the base of the half-done marble goddess

—all of the specifics of this planet, that
failed, at last, to suffice. And now

at this point, in a poem like "Dover Beach,"
the angst-filled 19th century speaker would

suggest that his lover snuggle closer against him, in their blanket
by the tide, and wriggle a little, risk some sand

up her beautiful ass (his 19th century vocabulary
would render this idea through different examples), since

her musk is good, and comfort is good, while overhead
the unfathomable "cosmic inflation" and "multiverse scenario"

and "string theory" of the 21st-century astrophilosophers
say that we're as chaff, or dust, or less, and the stars

themselves one day will sputter and die out. Anyway,
that's what I think on my walks. Poems are good,

and my wife's paprika-freckled skin is good, and they
return for their encores every night

on the lit stage of my personal mythology;
and they bow to the dark.

The Story of My Life

In astronomy, distance equals time; the farther away an object
is, the farther back it is in the past.

                                                    —Richard Panek

As if we could wield a shovel and dig
through outer space as down
the pitchy deepness or sedimentary rock
of prehistory-laden places like La Brea or Olduvai,
and sort that emptiness with a sift-screen,
with a professional's careful feather; and there
at the bottom black of the sky itself, we'd find,
and lift in our hands, an actual fossil
of light: a tusk, a horn,
some beautiful incurled ammonite, of alpha-light
we excavated out of the zeta-distance.

"At around nine we spotted the light of a fisherman's hut
at Sisarga, the last we could see on the European coast.
Soon distance weakened the feeble light, which we
began to confuse with the stars on the horizon."
—*Alexander von Humboldt, departing Spain in 1799*
for his South American explorations. How readily
the present moment is willing to extend itself,
back, to that earliest radiance
from which the atoms of "present" and "moment"
first began their long journey to Earth.

                            ∽

And once he reaches his destination von Humboldt says
"Our progess was often held up by having to drag
behind us from twelve to twenty loaded mules."
Cornering the junglier trails, the farthest of them must not
have even been in sight, their cargo of our own past lifetimes
—"animal skins and reptiles and fish in alcohol fixative"—
seemingly more distant because of this invisibility. My

fantasia is that, if I could join this laboring expedition and go
sequentially back through its mule-line
of baskets and crates, I'd find in each a minikin
of me from some essential moment . . . *here:* lip-synching
to Bonnie Raitt's version of Disney's *Dumbo's*
"Baby Mine" at the wedding . . . *here:* my mother is delivering
the oncologist's news (oh, such a coliseum of grief,
to fit in that tiny spangle on her lung!) . . . and *here:*
the bar mitzvah . . . *here:* I'm sloppily wrestled
out of her, as a haruspex might lift some obstinate, promising lump
from the entrails; then I'm set like a precious
rubicund gem in a bassinet in the breach births row . . .
until we reach the final mule's jogged-up box

of jumbled lizardbird compote, of salt bog
and trilobite, lightning and amino acids . . . *here:*
those microslices of my prostate
the urologist took can serve now as lenses
through which the sky is observed

to be the story of my life as told in constellations,
starting with *My Father Is Proposing*
to My Mother in a Canoe on the Lagoon
at Humboldt [yes, for the famous naturalist-explorer] *Park . . .*
I focus . . . I arrange his glowing celestial arms
so wide, they sign "the whole world," and I have her eyes
so literally de-lighted, they're a home to sudden novas . . .
1947 . . . as if I were the director of this
epic drama, and they were my stars.

"What Would Darwin Say?"

sounds like a party game—but no, I mean it
seriously, and ask it of various circumstances
often. Like today, when Nana told me the story, Anthony

and the meth, and baby momma number one he left
in the doorway, and the high-speed chase,
and Charles held the stash for him, so Charles
got collared and charged, and baby momma
number two with the stolen checkbook, Anthony
warrant, Anthony fake ID and coke in his boot
and baby momma number three with the VD
for a gift to their daughter, Anthony a total waste
of protoplasm, of motherlove, of human evolution.

॰

1859, and Darwin
steps around the duck pond to the low stone wall
he sits on in the nighttime when he wants
his daylong thinking to quiet. (He's "sensitive":
he visits physicians for "hydrophysick,"
he watches his skin record his doubts and ambitions
in rashes.) Tonight . . . he's finally published
the book—the book that will alter the world,
his final flower of decades of daylong thinking—
and now, more than ever, he needs the overbrimming
bowl of the moon to lave its pale calm
upon him.
                Meanwhile,
and not far away, that same fraught night, a lout
is going about the business of loutishness—it doesn't require
an AK-47, or a Web account to spew from; just a rock,
a simple rock, from the rubble of 1859 will do.
A contemporary of Darwin's—and fellow answers-questing
naturalist—Robert Chambers remembered this childhood scene:

"A coarse bustling carter used to leave his old worn-out
and much abused horses to die on the public green, and there,
without incurring reprobation, the boys amused themselves by,
day after day, battering the poor prostrate animals
with showers of stones till life was extinct."

❧

Tonight, a lucid full-moon night, I sit
on a stone wall, thinking—not intentionally
aping the Darwin I've set on a wall
in my earlier scene but, still, I'm here
and contemplating what seems to be the genes'
robust indulgence in combinatory
experiments. What else explains

last night, two women brawling on the floor at Deuces Hi
over Anthony—Anthony?—a batted-out tooth
and a raw red gouge in a breast—all this
for *Anthony?*—and a broken bottle smashing
so repeatedly into a head it looks like a waterfall
of glass, a waterfall tinted in blood,

while I happen to know that my friend Delora
is home, and providing her neighbor's daughter
a cello lesson. O moon, o moon,

that Darwin saw as an overspilling container of milk,
your wish is to pour over every kind
—as many of us as possible.

Dub

What I meant was that a squillion years of evolution slavered
in my body, thinking "pussy"—I was the current throbbing
edge of that continuum going back in time
past cytoplast and cilia to the first loose-field energy—
but what I said, and I said it directly
into her ear without the mediation of any room air, was
"I love you. God!—I love you." If I need to feel base
about that now, at least I represent only myself

while, sadly, government officials in my day, and daily,
spiel out such meretricious bunkospeak as makes
the rice grain shrivel inside its hull; and a man's
synaptic crackle turn away in disgust, to try
to lose itself in the radiant blasts of stars; and the very
tidewaters feel dirty for lapping anywhere near
the marble pillars of power. And yet at times our oily,
achey, striving flesh-selves have impossibly given

eloquence smacking of surefire unalloyed truth to the world:
"We are such stuff / As dreams are made on;
and our little life / Is rounded with a sleep" is
only one of many hundreds of lovely verbal planks
that Shakespeare lets us rest upon, across
the long, tormented nights. Or this,
from a science fiction adventure by Edmond Hamilton:
"'It will be a worthy battle,' Glevan said,

and grinned, 'We'll lose, of course. But proudly.
That's the thing.'" And also the skreel of cutlery
on bare bone Fanny Burney hears and feels
as her radical mastectomy proceeds (the year is 1811,
and all this fully conscious woman has for anesthesia
is a single glass of wine): you must seek out
this candor, read it for yourself: each word
a particular fire. And as for *how* our utterance succeeds

to higher levels than our resumés of failure and betrayal
would imply . . . I think I can tell you. Having astral-projected
and chrono-projected, along the trail of quantum mechanical pollen
in the firmament; and having done my deep-trance meditation
in the *chi* zone; having worn the invisible Lotus of a Thousand Petals
—a kind of "rapture *yarmulke*"—and so been granted a vision
of all the *yugas* in a *kalpa;* having thus been given admission
to the councils of Olympians . . . I've come to see that what

we say is how the gods arrange to dub their speaking
into mortal-talk. Not that I believe in literal "gods";
but *you* know what I mean, you know the times your words
have issued from a source that overgoverns and predates you.
When I say "the gods," I'm thinking less the deities of what
we call "the three major religions," and more the eternal,
fiercesome, foolish soap opera stars of the ancient Greeks.
Of course! That explains our nobility; but it also explains

this bar tonight. The slinky ho'-look honey in the silk faux-corset
bullying an accountant trying to broker a one-night deal
with her: dubbed. The long self-canonizing monologue
of the scabbed-up guy alone in the corner: dubbed.
The geek, the freak, a standardly vapid run of the meek,
the full caboodle and its babble-need. And me.
"I love you," I hear myself imploring. Look: look close:
my mouth is almost in perfect sync with the words.

Mapped

How deft we are at making it all
about the me. The ambulance,

that bears a man in artificial
cardiovascular pumping to his mysterious fate:

an overkill mnemonic for the baby aspirin
you forgot to take. The child's

surgery: one more excuse for you
to shine . . . all night, you were awake

with her; the sponges and the call button!
We can't help it, we can't fight the way

the brain is mapped around a central image
of itself around an image of itself. . . .

When the visiting curate swallowed his toast
in a talky, wrong-way gasp, his host

—eureka!—Charles Darwin fled the table,
wholly Charles-minded, to the alcove

where the earthworms turned in their jars,
and he spent the next half-hour thinking

about the mechanics of soil aeration,
while Emma was left to tend to the air

their visitor needed to breathe more calmly.
Where would we be, if Newton didn't heed

his self-set gravity, or Rosa Parks
the inward moral weight that kept her

sitting? Last week Katt and Tayvon
came to town. You'd think the swordfish begged

to die for the honor of being lifted
to his lips. The weather?—an ornament

to her beauty; in other moods, a rebuke.

Being Norman Dubie

She came (in the sexual sense). Or rather, she "came"
—that would be more accurate—for his benefit.
Also the way he'd met her family with
his friendly ("friendly") handshake
as mechanical as a piston.
Having heard them both, that night I walk the shore
unsure of who *anyone* is. The moon
is at its full, and so the waves in the bay
—which are normally like the rows of tiny rises
we see on a cheese grater—take a deep breath
and attempt to exceed the laws of their molecular containment.
Why *shouldn't* we easily be as fluid as this
medium that birthed us? Later on, at home:
a science fiction melodrama followed by midnight news.
The real problem isn't lizardmen from space
with the technology to pass for US senators.
The problem is US senators,
masquerading as human enough
to have your concerns at heart.
And of a shopkeeper, in a Joyce Cary novel:
"He moved his mouth just like a smile."

ↄ

One time I accepted an award for the poet
Norman Dubie. It wasn't "identity theft"
so much as "identity loan," and consensual
—so different from the poet
Patricia Goedicke considerately responding
to a weepy hard-luck email from some stranger
in Nigeria, and then finding her name
and her savings account appropriated by assholes.
This was after Leonard had died, and she was already
alone and frail, she was of large (and clearly
susceptible) heart. In fact, as the story shows,

susceptible self. Not that the "I" of anybody is
secure—our deepest slivers of identity are wont
to rise and nibble at the underside of the skin
as if begging to be hooked out. We love to stroke
the sleeves of other lives, where they're arrayed for us
on hangers on the rack of the local Select-A-Who.
No wonder we're easy prey, we so
collaborate with the hunters.
                              For a moment there *was*
a serotonin-boosting buzz in being
Norman Dubie, was a fountain of positive ions
in the brain; and—the acceptance speech
was only five minutes, but that was enough—
I understood the high involved
in the freedom of othercarnation.

                              ∽

"I"ons. Are there "you"ons? And are these essential
microparticles switchable (think Twain's
The Prince and the Pauper)? How could we *not,*
sometimes, insinuate ourselves into the psychescape
of other people?—we who are results
of the original inseminating of peptide bonds,
in Earth, by interplanetary dust: it's like the crest,
two comets rampant on a field of clouds of gas, for the entire
planet-family. But none of this addresses,
does it, the filth of the species, who burgled
Patricia Goedicke out of Patricia Goedicke one day
in the last year of her life. I knew her,
a little: a woman of grace and generosity
and intellectual appetite. I knew her and so
I can picture her—it's fanciful
but no less true—resigned to open
that final door, and enter another world

where maybe Leonard was, and certainly
the cosmos that she wrote about
in her poems with such appeal, and she would be nobody
and everybody, and all she had to do was sleep and dream
of a stone with her name engraved.

～

When a child makes a cup
from clay, you can often see his fingerprint
still in it—as if he isn't afraid
of saying who he is, or of you knowing,
of your lifting the cup by fitting
your finger into his own.

go north to work on the railroads. "Work"—that doesn't come close. Their sweat becomes another skin, as glistening as a frog's. At night they fall into sleep like boulders tipped into a black lake. This goes on for a year. But the money is good, and they each send a monthly tithe of it back home, and every Sunday night they phone their mother, taking their turn in line at the crew boss's office. "Doing good, Mama. Yes. No. How are you? How's Sissy? Yes, Mama. Love."

Roberto is the oldest. Tino is younger by eighteen months. And Tino always had, ever since he was a brat on the stoops, a kind of panther grace and panther musk that dizzied the ladies. He liked to drink. And when he drank he'd have ideas that life was meant to be more than a sledgehammer in a relentless drench of sun.

One Sunday Roberto tells his mother that Tino's throat is sore. The next week, that the foreman's sent Tino to town on important company business. Maybe she even believes it, at first. Maybe she doesn't suspect that Tino's taken up—and taken off—with a high-hemmed lowlife hoochiekoochie flirtygirl, and they've disappeared as completely as two dust motes pirouetted from light into shadow.

Or maybe she does suspect but, out of a motherly courtesy to Roberto's kindly fictions, plays along. "Oh, tell him: before bed, drink tea-and-honey. Oh, my Tino— I'm sure the foreman sees that little glimmer of good in him! Are there any nice girls up there, Roberto?" "Yes, Mama. Tino is seeing a very sweet schoolteacher lady, she works in Cedarville right nearby, I've heard her reciting poems to the children."

Fictions, like anything else, require fuel. Roberto must send his mother *two* tithes out of his monthly pay. And he must invest continually in the tales of Tino's absence. What next? Tino's a monk and he's taken a vow of silence. Tino's become a poet; he and his lady teacher-friend, they're off on a reading circuit at colleges scattered around the lakes.

The truth is, Tino was often truculently silent, unrevealing of his dreams and his simmering angers, a cipher. He'd stretch out under the blanket on the bunk bed as inert as an iron doorstop, as inscrutable as the carved god of some alien culture. What's troubling you, bro? (No response.) In his absence, Tino becomes more present than ever. In his fictional lives, he's more real.

And from that point on?—you can choose your own story. One—and it's the likeliest one—would be that the compulsion of Tino-X takes over Roberto's interior life completely. Tino in charge of the order's bee hives, moving in silence among that apiarian city's gridded rows, the buzzing so eternal that it *is* this city's silence; Tino overseeing the jars upon jars of honey that, in the rising sun, become the color fire must have when it's asleep and dreaming. Roberto has never one day in his life been religious, but he finds himself kneeling every night and muttering words he thinks might be the words a monk thinks, summoned from the quiet, at the foot of the throne of God.

Nor has Roberto ever read a page—of anything. But his brain (and this might not be unlike a hive accreting its honey) fills with poetry, the poetry of Tino-X. He sees himself at a lectern, raging—or would it be simpering over doves and hollyhocks? Or would it be the kind of gassy philosophizing he loosely links with the air over eggy mineral springs? He likes it. He starts to twiddle language around, to play with it—in his mouth, on paper, he plays with it. In the twilight consciousness just before sleep he finds himself saying *The geese are bound for somewhere. / Bound and gaggled.*

But then there's the story in which their mother dies. This news comes in a telegram from Sissy, ten words, that's it. This is the woman who'd wiped Roberto's snotty nose and runny ass and secretly bought him out of trouble when Delvecchio's thugs—excuse me, Delvecchio's "policymakers"—came looking for him with lead pipes over a matter of "pecuniary interests." The woman who'd saved his browning dried-up flap of foreskin, like a saint's toe, in a silver filigree box, to give as a keepsake to his bride one day, a day that's not yet come. His grief is intense, and his anger that Tino isn't here to share in the . . . Tino! It just now occurs to him: he won't be faking Tino's salary-tithe any longer, he won't be fronting for Tino's absence!

And yet this story finds him hooked. He can't give up those other lives by now. They make him more alive. Roberto is someone pounding a rail into the earth and keeping the company's trash-drunk hooligans in line. It isn't much and it sure isn't bait with which to woo a proper recipient of that foreskin reliquary. But Tino? Tino is an aviator, gone on record-breaking transatlantic expeditions. Tino owns a South Seas beach house, where a cloud of hula-hula girls and coconuts and sailfish is always providing the weather. Tino is off to deliver serum to a hospital in the frozen North— huskie sleds and igloos. How can he shut the door on these extra selves? The locals are gathered gratefully on the front steps of that hospital, under the radiant sky-bunting of the Northern Lights, delivering a cheer. *T! I! N! O!* they yell. If Tino ever returned now, how could Roberto give up this addiction?

And then there's the story where Tino returns, Tino and his trinkety over- eroticized inamorata. Tino the loser, the hard-luck fool, returns, having "struck it big." It's from "investments," he says; and then, the next day, "a ranch"; the next, "a dance hall business"—none of it rings true, although that last might be a sanitized revisioning of some dirtier truth. He wires money back home to Mama. Terrific: Tino, who never gave a shit, who couldn't tell you her birthday, Tino who was nowhere when one of the southtown Polack brothers knocked up Sissy . . . Tino's the hero now. Roberto's driving his millionth goddam spike and Tino's the family savior. Here, bro: Tino gives him a solid gold pocket watch with an eagle fob—a beauty! That night, Roberto walks to the middle of the Cedarville Bridge and flings the watch into the inky black, soliloquizing current.

Perhaps my favorite is the one where Tino never returns—but the woman does. The floozie, the strumpet—she comes back one day, bedraggled, borne into town on the breezes of loss. She doesn't know "where he went." One day she woke up in their room above the dance hall "and he was gone like he'd never been." She's carried a cheap valise—through God knows what adventures on the return trip—with his remaining belongings, to give to Roberto: a laceless pair of lumberman's boots; a solid gold watch with the crystal and both hands missing; an ivory tooth-picker in the shape of a dancer's gartered leg (the sexy spike heel serves as the pick); a fish-gutting knife in an oiled-cardboard sheath; a cardsharp's bowtie. She's weeping. It's all that she has, and she's turning it over to him, the older brother. Does he believe her? He looks: the front of her dress has been ripped by rough manhandling, and she's made a makeshift closure for it out of a fraying pair of lumberman's boot laces.

And in fact it isn't fair to say "the floozie." Whatever of her is in that word, well . . . there are other words Roberto discovers over the next few days. Patient. Tender. Parsimonious with button-thread and bacon fat, but generous with a kind of infectious, unselfconscious laughter. And she reads. To herself, of course, and sometimes to the children up in the Cedarville school, but also at night to him. She reads him poetry in the jitter of the oil lamp, and when the flame is near to its end she slips from her shift into ready sex as easily as a goose slips into water, and then she *is* a kind of poetry. The following spring, Mama and Sissy visit—they like her!—and Mama brings the silver box with the delicate filigree webbing its lid, and everyone has a laugh over that.

And these seem truly endless, in potential—these alternative lives—but dangerous as well, and officially frowned upon. You could get a ticket for exceeding the speed of truth. You could be issued a citation for not complying with actuality, for impersonating a likelihood. Cultural norms suggest prioritizing the people and the objects of the empirical realm—the ski lift and the burglar's mask and the nave and the breast and the hoof and the font and the architect's stencil—and not their ghostly correspondences tapping at our consciousness for admission from out of the realm of conjecture, and into the realm of reality. Ah, yes . . . but who doesn't enjoy a ghost story, or realize that we, too, were conjectural once, and rode here into incarnation on iffy winds of wish and will? Who doesn't feel a twin—Good-Me or Evil-Me, Me-X, Me-Raised-to-a-Higher-Power—sometimes yearning to separate out of the psychic matrix, to declare an independent presence in the world?

In the final story, Tino does return, alone, and with no explanations; he just picks up his hammer and bowl of soggy beans and shaving kit and begins again where he left off. Tino, yes. And yet: not Tino. Tino was left-handed. This one, the new one: right-handed, just like Roberto. And something almost mild and conciliatory guides him now. His silences aren't truculent as much as . . . thoughtful. What happened out there? *Who* happened out there? It's as if, somewhere in the deep of the woods, he entered a wormhole and came out reversed. Everybody notices it, the rail-thumpers, the camp cook, the saloon girls, even the unit boss who's usually above particulars. One day when they're in from a break at work, a woman who's been working the camp all year stares with a kind of wonder at him and says, "You remind me of someone." Tino looks up—not at her, at his brother. He says to Roberto, "All that time I kept thinking of you. I made up stories about you and I became those stories. I turned into you."

The Neutron Bomb

Since 2000, at least seven ghost ships have been found wandering the seas . . .
[including] an empty yacht found near Sardinia with half-eaten meals on
board.

—New Scientist

Of course when I read this I think of the cars,
undrivered, clogging up the nation's highways
in a helterskeltered, dented mess, that we've seen
in those cheesy painted vignettes of The Rapture: wavery
bodies spirited, like magician's scarves, to somewhere unknown,
with the physical transportation-pods of their former existences
left intact, and ticking down toward coolness
here, at what was supposed to only have been
the middle of their journey

                      . . . the equivalent
of what an observer might have seen as Dante,
who was famously "in the middle" as well, "of a dark wood,"
simply left this world for others, while behind,
on the path, the rucksack, cloak, and notebook
of his earthly travels remained, and in that dark place
seemed to suddenly grow darker
in abandonment.

               It may have looked as if
this little pile of belongings asked to serve him
as a magic anchor, capable of keeping him from flying
completely out of the planet's coordinates.
In 1849, on the eve of the long and unpredictable
journey from France to Egypt, young Gustave Flaubert
"left his study in Croisset exactly as though he were going
to return to it the next day—on the table a book
open at the page he had last read, his dressing-gown
thrown over a chair, his slippers near the sofa."
And yet in a way he never did return; a changed
and older Flaubert returned. Some wives, some husbands,
leave home in the middle of a meal,

for wine or cigarettes or milk, for something
so ordinary we can't imagine it
being the gate of their vanishing.

⌒

The Olmec . . . disappeared in the middle
of being the Olmec. A thousand years,
from 1400 BC to 400 BC, they ruled
in Mexico, creating Central America's first cities

and star maps and calendars and writing; today
we've uncovered the physical evidence of this prosperous civilization,
from its stubby, pure gold cheek-plugs
(of which four or five would easily fit
in your hand) and slivers of pottery as thin as phonograph needles,
on up to its pyramids (often crowned by a temple
[or maybe an observatory?]), its palaces,
its sporting arenas where games of deft precision were played
with gum-rubber balls and the luckless losers
forfeited their lives . . . and yet

this all stopped; all of these many thousands of people
stopped, without any sign of an intervening decline,
and simply disappeared. We don't know where they went,
or why, we don't even know their name for themselves:
it's the Aztecs who called them the people of Olmen,
"rubber country." Here

are the brooding Carnac stones, dating to the Neolithic, over
3,000 of them, some as tall as a man, and some as broad as an ox
("right now we have no notion of their purpose"), here are the supple figurines
that were carved in Mohenjo-Daro, 2,000 years before Christ
("the entire culture vanished; we may never know why"), here
the Minoan frescoes, here the wooden post on which

somebody from the Roanoke colony ("lost to history")
carved the name "Croatoan" before he (she?) irreversibly entered
Dimension X ("we have four major theories"), and here's
the brigantine *Mary Celeste* ("found drifting
in the Atlantic chop in 1872, no one aboard
and not one clue to their fate"),
and here are the plates of mutton and potatoes
left uneaten by the lighthouse keepers of Eilean Mor.
But the people . . . ? Do you remember the "neutron bomb"

our science boys were working toward during the Jimmy Carter years?
Enemy buildings would remain, still standing.
The highways, the conveyor belts, the water tanks
. . . remain. Only the people would be discontinued.
Only the people would be susceptible
             a roar   *a flash from the sky*
to oblivion
                    . . . and then, one day, if another planet's
paleontologists ever came here to study these remnant exostructures,
they might well assume the empty cars
they discover scattered everywhere, with lush, prolific grasses
growing through them, are the fossils
of some species: just the carapace left: the soft parts
and the soul, long gone.

                              ⌒

Nothing has been moved by an inch in Emily's bedroom
since they reported her missing. Mainly it's pinky pink,
the good-girl pink some parents think bespeaks
a fifteen-year-old girl. Her ruffled bed,
the teddy bear the size of an engine block,
her hair ties, the mirror . . . all pink. But one corner
—maybe an eighth of the room?—is a fuck-you
goth-punk-heavymetal-psycho-biker black;

the lifesize poster of her favorite group, Black Spittle, is black,
and the candles she positioned on either side are a satanic-ritual black,
and this one-eighth is the part of the room that functioned
as a teleportation device, and one night
Emily entered its wavelength and became black pixels
floating away away away. The shrine that she created
to those musicians is now a shrine to her.

In the Museum of All Things Goldbarth
you can see the Irving culture's weighty,
splayed-open Metropolitan Life Insurance Company
ledger book, that he fussed at nightly, trying to make
its figures tally nightly with our rent;
and, near it, the Fannie culture's set-piece scene:
an open pack of Lucky Strikes,
an Agatha Christie paperback, a meat loaf pan.
These artifacts are, for those who have studied the cultures,
emotional triggers: they imply a nexus of values
and a narrative as long as a life. But
the laugh of the one, the love-engendered nagging
of the other . . . ?
                    Because I've followed them, each,
to the cemetery and witnessed the closure-rain of dirt
on the casket lids, I can't claim that their vanishing
is mysterious in the way the seemingly incomplete arc of the Olmec
or the colonists of Roanoke is mysterious . . . and yet
not one of our metaphysicians can tell me, *really,*
where they've gone.

I'm sixty-seven.
                    Some days I survey the Albert Wing
of the Goldbarth Museum and shrug, and sigh. I'm thinking
of the collection of 1950s spaceship toys (they look
like a school of tropical angelfish, but of lithographed tin),
the pinup art (woo woo!), the manual typewriters

and the dimestore toys and the thousands and thousands
of books from sleaze to Talmudic studies
and . . . one day the Skyler culture
will hold an *extraordinary* yard sale.
                                          Some nights
I lay my head against my wife's reclining body
and hear a note—a single pure musical note
that she carries inside her while it flutters around
her ribs and through the tangle of fatty sheaths that coat her nerves,
in search of release. *I* think she's supernally special,
this woman; and yet I think we all have this note inside.
I read about it once in Sean Russell's novel *World without End:*
his hero passes "the partially opened doors of a ballroom"
and from them issues "the purest tenor voice Tristam had ever heard.
The song was familiar, an aria composed by Ramsay
for his great unfinished opera, and more moving for the knowledge
that it had been the composer's last work."
                                          That
final note, that wasn't intended to be the final note,
that rises out of a fatal interruption,
extravagant and rapturous. Soulfully rich and dolefully sad
and complicatedly rapturous.

"Try the selfish,"

someone said—the host
with a cigar like a Chevy's exhaust?—or his wife
in the dress with enough gold trim for a room
of antiquities at the Vatican? Anyway,

I was thirteen, and fresh from a house
where the limiting laws of *kosherkeit* were kept,
and that's what I heard, and that's
indeed what I tried, and so forever

this first sensual, taboo, awakening
taste of shrimp that turned my own tongue
inside-out to something that might hunch
across the sea floor, is connected

in my memory with wanting more,
uncaring of any consequence . . . and it stayed
with me the first time that I ate a woman
—a *shiksa,* at that—attentive

to the selfishness of slower,
faster, no, no, over *there,* yes!,
having promised the night
would be all about her, and pleased

to please those flavors and their pliancy;
and pleased in an aesthetic way
to see her sleeping afterward in exactly
the perfect curl of a shrimp. And you

perhaps don't like this poem: its free verse
or its narrative or the way it uses
gender or the heavy-handed
word-play of its title.

Like I care.

I wrote this for me.
And as a tribute to the shells we bear
and break from; and a tribute to
the ocean that she carried in her body.

OTHER LIVES

Encyclopedia Brittany

It happened again last night, my neighbor
Brittany says: the quantum mechanical universe
and the terms of her divorce ganged up
"like bad cop, bad cop" and anything certain
and central "went gazonkers," and she was falling
through a madhouse of quasars and parsecs
and lonely-girl-scotch-on-the-rocks . . . and what she did
(as efficacious as any of her prescription meds) was

take her last scotch into the dark like a torch
in her hand, and under the face of that grand quizmaster
full moon, and his honors class of stars, she started
reciting *viviparous, chasuble, money shot,*
reticule, rhizome, riata, pierrot, szekler, crested tit,
a tipsy mantra of terms
that indicate the knowledge of a particular expertise, "it
quickly neutralizes the chaos." And it does. It comforts

me to witness Sexxie roll a blunt (with the concentration
and dainty touch of someone, somewhere, curatorial
rerolling a sixteenth-century Japanese scroll) and later on
decode BBBJ and DATY off
her online escort ad—the way it also comforts me
to know that OPERA (Oscillation Project
with Emulsion-Racking Apparatus) followed over 16,000
neutrinos fired from Switzerland to Italy. And yes,

I've experienced Brittany's *tsooris*—haven't you?
I've often walked some rimroad of the night
that led me straight to the edge where everything
—love and friends and poems and conscience—teetered
fatally over The Long Fall Past Returning. And I've clung
to Brittany's cure-all there. Someone knows what a finial is,
a manticore, a belvedere, a merkin, a firkin,
a tonsure, a peetweet, a jerkin, a universal joint.

Her One Good Dress

wedding *and* funeral

22

[Teenagers] grabbed the [swan] when he came to the defense
of his mate, held him down, stabbed him, and cut off his
head with a hunting knife.

—The Rockland Journal News (1994)

Now everyone will write a poem for these
unfortunate birds. Their song will continue to haunt

the language that memorializes it, their song
a long—a hundreds of miles long—complaint

across the cold dark lakes and the wheel of sky
they traveled to arrive at death

by brutal hands. The poems
will say that every feather was perfect. The poems

will picture the silhouette of their paired-up gliding:
an elegant 22. And now there isn't a "rush of wings"

or a "plaintive call" that won't be, justifiably,
repeated in books and online and at gatherings

of the kind that understand both beauty
and victimhood. But who will write the poem

for those boys, and see that the twisted lines
in their minds began as straight

as anyone's, and will see that their dreams
are only the corrupted version of anyone's,

and will say that their fetid crabapple miscreant hearts
are as precious as anyone's.

"If you saw even the first rocket take-off for Mars,

you'd pay little attention to it if you had to stand in a cloud of
mosquitoes to watch it."

—John D. MacDonald

There are worlds that have a dozen moons, the shadows
of a person look like fanned cards
or like wind-whipped reeds; and there are worlds with orbits that trace
a figure-8 onto the void of space, those people have
four skies by Earthly standards; and worlds
of perpetual, ubiquitous aurora borealis; and worlds
. . . but my point is, on one of the worlds a mother

is lifting the newborn to one of her four engorged nipples
and seeing, really *noticing* for the first time, a splotch,
a misplaced bindi-dot-of-a-splotch, beneath
the infant's chin, with a barely-there scrim of crust around it,
a sign of the "lava disease" (it begins as a mole,
then spreads until the entire body is covered in corrugation
that looks like bark or hardened lava) she's just read about

on her wrist-screen stream, *if* that's what this dot
even is, and she stares at it, stares at it, stares at it
as a yogi might stare at a mandala until he *enters*
the mandala and lives out every possible mandala-lifetime
in its concentric circles . . . my point is, she barely
looks at that amazing plasma-geyser sky
in its psychedelic glory . . . no more than does the lover

who's in (or entered by) the other lover (it doesn't matter
which, for my point), and saying "Oh my furred soufflé!"
(except it's *that* planet's concept of "soufflé"), "My
puissant éclair!" and performing a sexual calisthenic
of extensible, deviant pleasure so intense, the room
disappears, the grove of float-trees disappears,
and the sky is non-existent . . . so too, with my friends

and yours, and time. I passed a house last night
in which the constant screaming was a weather
people were born to, and grew up in, and died from. O,
we were eating out the minute, we were praying to
and nursing and flaunting and fucking and buying and oil painting
and gossiping about and fervently scratching the itch of the minute
—we didn't even notice the years.

Of the Generality

Licking it, up that close now, it
was different. Another example: the present moment
is larger than all of the past. One more:
your daughter's lupus versus some
far country's genocide. Of course examples aren't proofs;
but tell me who would doubt the generality?
Proximity is everything. This afternoon

a vee of geese blots out the sun—is louder,
and traveling more rapidly. At night the ocean goes
to where it laps against the lowest stars.
Because of her weeping, her spitting at them, and the intimate
flowering musk of her pee, the hostage
in a corner of the guerillas' shack is suddenly
so much huger than their cause.

Silences

Cassie is at her mirror, applying
her Saturday-hot-night makeup
in vigorous—*no;*
her son is deaf
and what she's doing tonight is
practicing American Sign Language.

～

An ancient Roman garrison.
The archaeologists find a golden bugle
many layers down. Around it, a scatter of golden coins
—the perfect notes it's hitting.

Etc.'s Wife

The story is: he peed his seat in English 101, and Dash
the security guy was a half hour late so by the time
the chair was wheeled down the hallway, past the sumptuous
regalia of stars on a poster for the Astronomy Department,
and Marine Biology's scroll of squiddly life forms,
to whatever sanctum of fumigatory rehabilitation
the college reserved for its chairs, the student in question
had already been expelled . . . not for the loosening
of his bladder, of course, but when he was questioned
about this by the Dean of Squeamish Interrogation,
he'd offered up immediately that he'd "been drinking
overly," and so was in admitted violation of the policy
on alcohol consumption and, although the chair returned
in a day, the student never did. To understand this

story *really,* though, we need to understand a story
is smoke in the wind, when the air is autumnally rich
with burning leaves and the contending scents of an outdoor market:
shishkabob, patchouli, grand aromas from the curry booth . . .
there *isn't* any one exclusive storyline. In fact, it turns out
he was mildly retarded, part of why his urination
couldn't be controlled, and so he speedily offered up that drunkenness
as the offending cause: it made him "one of the guys,"
it reinvented him, in *his* mind, with a cool excuse,
and not his old congenital embarrassment. And yet, by the time
his mother picks him up, the sour smell of defeat and humiliation
is more rank than the seat of his pants; then, these two vanish . . .
smoke in the wind. Now through his window, the Dean of Etc. is idly

observing their car drive off as he waits for his wife—as usual,
late. Of course: she's happily been aroused and rumpled
in the utilities room with Dash. *That* ancient story. And
sometimes she's simply wandered the halls alone, a little
lost—both *in* and *to* herself. When she studies the poster
of stars and void and solar explosions frozen by Hubble
into light-years chalices and opened roses, mesmerized
by this . . . she suddenly thinks the story is with the fish,
those weirdly fringed and hinged and chandelier-bodied
lives of marine biology. And when she studies the fish, deep
in *their* deep . . . then the story is with the stars,
the gassy helices and butterflies of radiance, that take her
out, and further out, beyond the idea of "person," and beyond
a "wind," or "air" itself, or any story we make of them.

Detective / Woody / Sci-Fi

One clue in the mystery novel is that the husband
is drawn to young boys. The darkness
separating him from them is like the outer space
between two planetary systems that are likely
to collide with fatal results. Although he really does
love his wife. Well, most lives aren't that
disastrously convolute; and yet, as we can verify
from any one day in our own familiar worlds, it's
never quite upfront and easy. Woody Allen says
"The heart knows what it wants." Although
the head isn't always informed of this. Life is always
a "mystery": the books shelved thus are merely us

times us; they take their power not from difference
but resemblance. That's what love is, in a novel:
it's your neighbor-boy's unraveling ménage à tois; and Inga's
congruent loves for her children and for most any guy
with a baggie of crack and jail tatts; it's Jesus duking it out
in you with Buddha; and it's never, ever free of complication.
In a science fiction novel, a starfaring alien race
evolved from plants is searching for a new home
solar system: their sun is dying, and so their instruments
are tuned to identify chlorophyll-friendly planets.
Earth, for instance. Their intent is to destroy us.
Their hunger is innocent: light and sugar.

World

You shake it, and a spherical confusion
of white—a dazzle—lifts and settles, lifts and settles

on the lovely miniature world inside
a snow globe: but there is no market

for dust globes, even though the Great Depression
is worth commemorating, with tiny men

and women and their tiny, tired persistence
on a long road, carrying babies and pans, and earth

the dirt, and Earth the planet, whirling against each step.

"The Pulses

and the Minuses" is only one example,
though a favorite. And the extra *t*
in "Putrify Your Water," or the missing *e:*
"Relive Your Stress." As usual it isn't

funny once it's us and not some verbal
analogue: a single gene gone wrong
(or, more extreme, a single gone gene)
and it's Amy Lazer's very real

and fatal disorder. I remember stories
of her mother, every morning, rolling up
like yarn the gluey strings
that webbed her daughter's lungs. And also

Kelso in the last stage of what AIDS did
underneath his raw-meat skin
("a foreign lesionaire," he said, the wit
a flicker of his earlier panache) until

there wasn't Kelso-ness below
to feed on any longer. What I mean is
this: the small things that we need to love,
we need to love as if they were epic;

as if they held great portions of the oceans,
as the glaciers do. The small things
that we need to fear . . . let's tremble
as if they were meteor collisions, even if

they fit on a microscope slide.
Well how's *that* for didactic! But our days
are sick with error, and need
a dose of the prescriptive. "Pulses,"

by the way, is the right word in that title
of a medical text I quoted for you.
But who misread the penmanship
enough to misprint "Viruses"?

Lepidopteran

" . . . there is a kind of moth / here on the earth /
that feeds only on the tears of horses."

—Malena Mörling

Another moth will sup on only
the tears of a deer.
The bird that lives on only the ticks
of only one kind of rhinoceros.
The fish that swims from birth to death
self-caged in a single anemone.
On one day we might call this limitation . . .
on another day, devotion . . .
depending on how we feel about
our invention of monogamy.

∽

Ghosts:
they wander—some of them merely slipping
down the church stairs with the bonelessness
of spilling water, and some of them
over miles of moon-dabbed moorland—
but they never philander.
Ghosts: they're faithful
to only one body.
But here I'm talking marriage

when I started out wanting to write about moths.
And maybe I can address both
simultaneously in Alana and Digger.
Nothing stopped their love war: they would argue
at the neighbor's daughter's christening as easily
as in the silts of last-call at their biker bar,

Big Belly's. "Argue" isn't close:
they were predatory, born for the chase
and the kill, there was no implication of shittiness
of the soul too out-of-bounds for them, and each
was slim, but grew fat, feeding
on the other's weeping.

⌁

It was like watching a kind of fatal ballet.
He'd tumult from the wings
to center stage, all braggadocio
about his little fuckarounds with L and T; and
she'd recoil, I'm sure in woe, but also to accrue
an extra wind-up for the pitching forth
of S and W into his face. Eventually
it would turn physical; I've seen what an edge
of beer-bottle-shard could do along his cheek.
And yet he'd come back to her, he needed her,
he needed *this*. As she did. Needed even the scorch
of his cigarette on her left breast. She would leave
to stay at Alice's . . . but return in a week, would leave
with every stale muffin and t-shirt . . . but be back,
for more, away . . . return . . . away . . . return. . . .
Yes, like a moth and its flame.

⌁

Some are tiny and pale:
the cabbage moth is like a single ampersand
that's flown its way out of a footnote.
Others have the span of a skillet,
and are marked with whorls that rival those

of the peacock, or the Great Red Spot on Jupiter.
They fly, with a tremolo flutter;
and are powdered, like biscuits;
are feather-antenna'd.
They really aren't like us at all.
And one more difference,
the central one.
The moths don't cause the tears.

Street Signs

and when the tribe ran low on iron arrowheads
they mounted their war ponies   O, it was sunny
and clear and Essie revved her motorcycle and sleeked it
over the back roads onto the freeway   *and then they charged*
the enemy camp, and rode "all-crazy-with-the-war-gods"
into its maw, its living waiting slicing edges   and
skidded full-front at the twenty-seven-car pile-up,
and deftly started to speedsnake through its chaos,
but was thrown, and was run over
twice, without ever losing consciousness   *and didn't*
ever swerve, but kept on straight at the enemy eyes
and the enemy weaponry   and her pelvis was shattered
at five separate points, her jaw was broken,
her teeth were pushed through her gums,
and an arm and a shoulder and a hand and a leg
were broken, and her skin at those places
was pretty much gone   *and they yelled* Hei hei *to Death,*
and were shot by the enemy arrows, again and again,
so this way those who survived rode home
with the iron points they so coveted, and they plucked these out,
so many that the raid was considered successful

❧

11 p.m. I meet Evan at a Denny's. If he can leave from here
by midnight he'll pull into Boulder at 8 a.m.
and get to spend a day with Essie,
between her bouts of physical and psychological
therapy. And then drive back. How weary
he looks already, before his forty-hour-turnaround
mission of love has even started: there's no coffee
in the world, I think, that's up to the task
of jumpstarting his pallor. We joke, but it's true:
in the recentmost photos, just three weeks
from the day of the wreck, Essie looks more vibrant

113

in her medical techno-netting than the two of us do
in Denny's bleaching wattage. If anything,
Essie is a certified secular miracle: just three weeks,
and she's out of bed and hopping on the one good leg.
She's painting with the one good hand.
She's peeing out good urine with her good and timely bladder,
and she threw up after eating a meal of Thai food
with her temporary teeth, and it was good,
so gastrointestinally good, to feel
the forceful riled muscles
of that mechanism working!

&

At a corner near here are two conflicting street signs.
One is a U-shaped arrow: turn around, return.
And one is an arrow pointing straight ahead
inexorably. This last must be
what the 19th-century Czech story writer and journalist
Jan Neruda witnessed as he slept in the bed
where his father "lay dying": he woke
and looked, and looked, he says "I kept studying
how a man dies"—that one-way journey
occurring inches away from him, probably touching him,
as the rest of Prague resolved back into daylight.
And my wife's friend S's husband R:
the one-way ticket: impeded a bit by the chemo, yes,
but just as irreversible as the destiny
of an avalanche in motion. And my friend J's brother:
pancreatic: nothing, not even the "trial drug,"
is going to lead him back to who
he was before the creepers started spreading
through his body. It's because of this

linear physics that we marvel at her
ferocious disobeyance of its rules, our sassy saint-girl
of the U-turn. Evan's back—instead of drained
he's reinvigorated by visiting her. He says
the bad arm looks like melted plastic but
the rest of her . . . "it was almost as if I could see scars
healing in front of me," the moonscape pucker
smoothing over even the course of one day. She's out
of her murmurous nest of life-support contraptions
and can lift and swivel her new-done hips enough
to be wheelchaired over to the park.
                                        He says
she lay there on the freeway and deliberated whether
to live or die—"and it was so close, but after a long time"
she decided to trust the necessary pain
of her recuperative genius. Evan says
(although not in these words exactly) she rode
with a wild abandon toward the camp of Death,
she circled its rim, she said "*Hei*
hei, I spit on you,
hei, I piss on you, Death, I con you
out of your fatalmost arrows and now they're mine,
I pluck them out like flowers"—shaking Death's own arrows
in Death's own face with the fuck-you finger lifted
unharmed and defiantly, *hei,* on her good hand.

> "Who carries a telephone book with them
> when they are running from a war?"
>
> —Ammon Shea, *The Phone Book*

A Chinese man, Chao Lu, has memorized
pi's first 67,890 digits. The tycoon
J. P. Morgan found and bought and possessed
—that was the crucial part, *possessed*—
his own three Gutenberg Bibles, out of a known
forty-eight. A certain person's passion may burn
completely contained inside another person—I would say
that was true of my father, regarding my mother.
Another person . . . it may take a thousand flames
inside a thousand nineteenth-century fishing lures
to burn his passion completely. A thousand
luridly painted plaster icons of saints. A thousand
days in the lab, in search of a cure for cancer.
My name is Yann Mharboush, and in the city

I called home, I oversaw the organizing of,
and selected the font for, and the cover for,
its first comprehensive telephone book. It
wasn't just "pride of accomplishment." No.
My friends were all in it, women I'd kissed
in their secretmost creases were in it, as were
my enemies, and the places where, before
the bombs completed their rain of terror, a wife
could stop to buy those "baby's ears," the pastries
made with Cognac we were famous for . . . what
better relic to take? So I took it. And one night
when I stumbled over a dead dog's body, automatically
clutching the book to my chest in shit-pants fear,
it stopped a bullet.

Summary: Kinetic vs. Potential

In 1796 Elias Henshaw, who had never smoked
a cigar or a pipe or ever taken a dram of spirits
or even entered a spirited altercation, burst
spontaneously into flame—no heat source
anywhere nearby—and such was the ravenous
ferocity of the fire that, despite his friends' alacrity
with a ladled-out barrel of rainwater, he
was soon reduced to a stack of greasy ashes,
disturbing to view and rancid to whiff.
In 1854, Rebecca Norris the same. Wen Fu
and Israel Lodz the same. A famous scene in Dickens
describes the phenomenon. In 2003 an infant
five months old named Shylene Washington, in a room
devoid of the tiniest spark, a room that was,
if anything, dry and chill according to witnesses,
turned—*snap!*—into a burning, melting
shapelessness that would fit on a christening pillow,
and pool, and cool to a rubbery mass with only
a few charred bones to hint that once this thing
possessed an identity. The annals of human mystery
bear hundreds of such instances—not that

any friend of mine has succumbed, or I'll wager
any of yours, or any friend of those friends', or even any
stranger I've seen, not at the salon, or the governance meeting,
the strip club, the news room, the sacristy,
or at marriage counseling—no more than my own
so-very-willing-to-be-credulous (though not
irrational) eyes have witnessed even one of the thousands
of reported saucers skimming like Scottish curling stones
over sheet ice, buzzing low like electric clippers
over the wheat, or sometimes landing on a highway in an air
their subacoustic hum makes green (or purple) (or streaked
throughout with snakes of light), and green (or gray) (or gray-green)
beings emerge, "the credible witnesses include an Air Force pilot

and a sheriff," "a van of tourists," "everybody on the plane,"
although not me, nor have I seen the ghosts or the yeti
or one sprung werewolf hair from a cheek, and yet
the testimony to such things is a clamor so unending, that
the seeds of these extremities *must be* deep in us, in all of us,
and anyway "the absence of proof," as Carl Sagan has pointed out,
"is not the proof of absence"—an exemplification of which
might be (remember the marriage counseling?) my friends

Shalimar and Abel, who will sit in front of their mediator
an hour at a time like milk glass figurines, so
pale and still, although you know their subatomic bonds,
if broken, would—like anyone's—release the same hellfire
that devastated Hiroshima and Nagasaki, yes, they host
their weekly dinner parties with unruffleable calm, and yet
you know their molecular makeup, the electrochemical
selves inside their selves, can't differ much from that
of the neighbor who kneels unashamed in the street to conduct
her conversations with angels, arguing, crooning, spitting, giving
off the blaze-light of a torch. A woman
I knew once pointed coyly to her clit (yes, there's a background
story that really isn't a part of this) and told me something
I've always imagined being uttered by Doctor Tulp
in Rembrandt's famous "anatomy lecture" painting, as he draws
his viewers' attention down the length of a laid-out body
that's skinned to its raw, pink, fatty abundance. "Just
because it isn't burning
doesn't mean it's not a candle."

Left Behind

Among the many curiosities . . . [is] a stupefied, beached fin whale
straddled by 15 inquisitive monks.

—from a review of *The Whale Book* in *Discover*, January 2005

In my earlier life I visited a brothel, and there
were women who fit that gaudy and high-hemmed life

as true as a smooth leg fits its hosiery—but
others wore the look of some of fate's sad misconsignments,

and their smiles felt like cracks in glass. The same
among the whalers (for the brotherhood often apportioned us

into the world, to do our work): the ones who seemingly
were born to clamber rigging, and the ones in whom a fire

of unbelonging would color the back walls of their eyes:
no grog could douse it. Thus it was with me,

in the monastery, for all of those years; the light
through an oriel window in the chapel's western-facing wall

would touch whatever other brothers walked across
its oblongs as if equal light rose out of them

to meet it. I felt no such thing, I radiated
no such thing, although I tried and duly loved those people

and their life. But I was . . . similar, as opposed
to the same. A rupee in with the pence. And so that day

I never returned. It wasn't intentional—not at first.
But there are flies that are proportioned to the death

of a whale, as others are assigned to the punier deaths;
a hundred thousand of them, and together

they made the universe-buzz of electrical wires
passed through the fields of stars. I heard it deep

inside my teeth. It seemed to own me. That,
and the sun (this was late August), and a stench

so rich, the air around it wavered like the air around
hot tar. I grew faint. And instead of walking away

across a beach where there was neither shade nor softness . . .
in a daze, and while the others were admiring

the corrugated flukes . . . I climbed inside the lips,
I lay down to rest on the rubbery slate of the tongue.

And then they left. They must have called for me,
and searched, and were puzzled. But finally they left

in the three small shallops; and when I awoke
it was evening; I was alone; and I understood

that I should stay here; and I have,
these eighteen years. I am the voice

of a gullet that properly should be beyond
all voice now, and I go about the office of this prolongation

seriously. But how and why, they ask—for on occasion I do
have visitors. Some fancy me the Holy Man, and would I

set my left hand like a starfish asleep for a minute
on the camembertish pudge of her infertile mons or his

distended sack. For most, however, I'm
the Caretaker (they must imagine my rounds with a sponge

and sudsy ammonia, scrubbing the great bone stanchions sleek of fungus).
In all truth—it was *the whale* that cared

for *me*. Example: early on—before the long dissolvent
rains and verminry began, and left the clean

freestanding galleries you see—the whale fed me.
Chandeliers of meat gigantically clotted the ceiling length,

and one especially succulent organ—just about the size
and height above me of a boar's head on a hunter's chateau wall—

provided oily slivers of nourishment for a full year: it
was like a grant. And I could feast, and dream, and scrabble

ever farther inward: Brother Hermit Crab. And this is where
their easy allusions to Jonah fail: I didn't want out,

I'd willingly expatriated myself, and my
new mother country—steppe and tundra, scree and veldt—

awaited me with intricate sufficience: hanging gardens,
gullies, weirdly feathered ridgebacks, and those haunted plains

where the ghosts of the billion krill still keened
their absence: each was less than a mosquito whine, and yet

this belly held *a ton* of krill: *a ton*
of otherworldly music. Do I ever miss the gladness

in a human touch? The sex scent in an alcove
of the brothel? Or the whaling sailors' rowdy camaraderie?

O yes. But regret is like shoes that I leave
outside, on the sand, so as not to mar the floor

of my home. And by the creed of the monastery,
satisfaction in one's own life can rise

to the level of sin. If so, I will need to repent a minute
for every minute I live. If only you could see me . . . !—when I enter

my encampment in the mouth, I sing a footnote
to the operatic transatlantic coo-and-boom of whalesong

he once poured forth prodigiously into the currents;
when I dance like a dandy, down and back

in the gutters of him, I trace the muscle pulleys
that rigidified the thick spar of his pleasure; when I dance

about the brain case, I'm a living graph
of whale hallelujah; when I kneel

in the skull, and watch the sky-shine wheel across
those empty eye holes, I'm inside a dome

as wonder-filled as any sacred space on earth,
and fit for a cathedral.

As the World Turns

It's *not* used in our neurological way, but
there it is, in Dickens's *Bleak House*, suddenly:
"ganglion." We thought it a twentieth-century word,
and current into the twenty-first, but there he was,
in 1851, in London at Tavistock House—in a hand
of that city's genial springtime sky as it was dealt out
through the fanlight, and then working on into the night
by a gas jet—emptying out the universe
that was folded into his brain, each chittering jackass session
of Parliament, and every ill-made stilton that's
as rubbery as a pessary . . . and there it is,
in the midst of all this, a "ganglion" of streets
. . . it feels almost like effrontery. In chapter 40,
"refrigerator"—referencing the chilly hauteur
of Sir Leicester Dedlock, baronet—depriving us of our claim
to that word by a century. This tunnel of prior use
is evidently aeons long: we've turned up whole teeth
from the Iron Age (examples no more umbering
or crumbled than the teeth some dentist might have pried at
just this morning) delicately drilled,
and sometimes filled too, with what's obviously an urge
toward preservation, and a tool kit that we'd find
not unfamiliar. *We imagine we're the first:*
but we're not. And the opposite lesson
(or would it be "the corrective lesson"?) is also there
in *Bleak House*. Lady Dedlock dies. That reigning crown,
that coolly sculptural beauty, of the fashionable world . . .
and so iconic in her resolute establishings
of taste, that it's impossible to think of her as lessening
in any way, or liable to succession . . . here, on page 808
in the famous Nonesuch Press edition, death
has grown across her body like the damp fur of a mold,
like a kudzu of window frost; and there,
in the dank of a pauper's graveyard, Edith Summerson cradles
her mother's corpse. Before that, Jo dies; after,

Richard Carstone. Nemo. Gridley. Krook. The author himself
is not immune (who could conceive it, having seem him emote
like sun-coronas, reading from the stage?); he slipped
unwillingly into his final day on June 9, 1870,
while the planet—with its yam crops and torn love notes
and monsoons and plankton and Senate bills
and cerebral palsy and fine champagne in pails and
inveiglements of every sort—kept turning, and therefore
turning away. There were other novels, later; other novelists.
My friend S., for example. Husband, tennis player, writer
of stories like Amazonian torrents stirring
occasional precious gems, and—news from only Monday—
bearer of lymphoma, which was speckled through
his X-rays like a dill. I don't believe that
he can be replaced, but which of us can. Well, none of us
and all of us is the answer and the lesson
from the planet's veldt, the planet's roofs, the planet's ganglion of streets.
We imagine we're the last: but we're not.

A Gold Coin of Kumaragupta I (Minted AD 415–450)

One one side is a massive, handsome stallion
so packed with muscle, it looks as if
it could pull, on its own, a palace
or a fortress from its foundations—and this horse
the king himself would have killed in front of an audience,
with a gold knife, as a proof of his legitimacy:
the ritual is pre-Hindu and so, by implication,
the right of the king to his power is rooted
unshakably in the First of Days. On the other side

of the coin: the Hindu goddess Lakshmi,
naked, rounded everywhere a female body *can*
be rounded, and in the size of about
a penny she says that the gift of sensual pleasure
is a holy thing. And so one side is a sign

of political stratagem; one, the deific. One side,
ancientdom beyond memory; one,
the overpresiding religion of the moment. Of course
one thinks now of the octopus

—when it senses a potential mate is watching,
that side of it pulses an extraordinary psychedelic display
of oh-wow color; the half that's still concerned with the rest of the world
continues on, in its dully inconspicuous
safeguard camouflage. And you,

my friend with the brain stem and the neocortex
pulling toward their quarrelsomely adversarial poles, you
with the office-self and the dream-self? Alice says

the story goes that her grandfather Isaac
was a stern, proud man, a Russian Jew
of indomitable bearing, and in his house—and widely known
in the local annals of awe—he had a dining table
of vista and gloss to match his outsized personality. One day
the Cossacks came. "We're taking your table." "Yes sir,"
he said—for who would refuse the Cossacks?—"it will be ready
for you in twenty minutes." And when they returned,
there it was, a pile of axe-hacked splinters,
the whole thing. "Okay, take your table."
Like the moon. This was its other face.

I Remember the Look of My Ex-Wife Sitting Quietly in the Window on a Certain Day

What did she look like? Everyone knows: the swanlike neck,
the dark, doe eyes, the high, noble forehead on a delicate-
featured head, crowned by a towering blue headdress.

—Sharon Waxman

Nefertiti means "The Beautiful One Has Come"

and this rendition of her was sculpted out of limestone
in the workshop of Thutmose
about 1340 BC

and having survived the subsequent era's
destruction of most of the other sculptural references to her
—essentially, the destruction of her sisters—

she was excavated in 1912
her beauty as so often happens immediately argued over
by Egypt Britain France and Germany
all demanding ownership

and was ceded to Germany
there to go on display in 1923 in Berlin
although the international arguing continued

and remained there in Berlin as the Hitler war machine
was pieced together
and remained there as the tanks and missiles and gas chambers
left the blueprint stage

and in 1939 because of the war was taken
to shelter in a salt mine in Thuringia

her one good eye with the inlaid iris
and the one that had left the workshop blank
so many thousand years before

surrounded by walls and ceiling and floor
of salt salt salt salt salt salt

all of the stuff of weeping
and not one tear.

We Focus on Love, When It's Death;
We Focus on Death, When It's Love; Etc.

A third-rate magician still, by definition,
serves up magic. This one's shlepping his card tricks
table-to-table around the third-rate nightclub;
even the big-nose shmo who's also going
table-to-table quietly heckling Galacto the Great,
and even the watery drinks and the sour, imposing air
in a conspiracy of moodiness can't similarly sour
or water down the crowd's amazement as,
with a fanning-out of his cards, Galacto showily
slows his rapid-fire patter and begins to reveal the face
of the raised-up central card from out of that arc, and
—eek!, *huh?,* lo, three golden eggs impossibly pop
from his mouth, that he nattily scoops up, with a flourish,
in a cap-from-out-of-nowhere. The trick of course

is what the fraternity of prestidigitators calls "diversion"
—insisting glitzily on A, while Z
finagles under the table. For example, all this while
the poem is really about the woman who left
her overpriced drink and her bantam-wit blind date
at the club, and slunk back home on the last bus of the night,
to curl in bed, in her lifelong feeling of loss
—her old familiar hurt—the way that soldiers in Siberia
hacked their way inside their horses' bellies, curled up
in that raw heat for the night: it wasn't pretty, but
it saved them from the outside world. And nothing now
is going to divert her from her clinging to this one thing
that she knows so well and that, by its very
consistency, is a comfort. Not the clef note

made of a single winding hair, inside the family Bible.
Not the cop car only one block over, with its stuttering
blue light. Not the rust. Not the dew.
Not the jasper and cornelian, or the marzipan.
Not the sleeping moan in the oboe, waiting to awaken.
Not the parade confetti—in either its light, balletic descent
or its final bedraggled tangle. Nothing will move her
concentration away, not even—perhaps *especially* not even,
it's so inhumanly far—the overarching splendor
of the galaxies, that mysterious script of pinpoint fire
written across the night. For others, the opposite
is true: in 1768, the astronomy-crazy
British Royal Society discovered that one of its clerks
had embezzled its treasury of 1,500 pounds—or,

as one Fellow put it, while they "had been attentive
to what is to pass in the Heavens," the clerk
had "run away with our Money upon Earth."
—A precursor to the big-nose shmo
who's picked a dozen pockets or so,
table to table, shmooze by shmooze, who came
from out of nowhere and is halfway to Nebraska by now.

The Clothes

Now listen. Listen up! I want Estrella
to come onstage with weeping all over her, every way
except tears: I want the weeping scurrying
inside her like bees in a rotted-out wall, or water
welling up in the ground that the city authorities categorize
as toxic: *that* kind of underground tears.
And more *squirrels!* Hey, some shmuck-of-a-gofer not doing
nothing—you! do you hear me, skinny?—get the squirrel man
to come to the squirrel delivery door
with a few more cages. Say sixteen. Augoosto:
walk more like a robot. No . . . no . . . *there!*
Maurice: I said mousse in your hair, but not a half-a-year
of cow-gunk from the Ganges River. Estrella: . . . no, wait,
Augoosto: clank clank clank! You got it,
boobeleh, Mr. Method Actor? Good . . . good . . . hotsy totsy!
Estrella, pull at your gorgeous hair
like bell ropes in a tower
of weeping—that would be . . . *emblematic!* I want
to see your hands like rival suitors
crawling up Rapunzel's tumbled-down ladders of tresses.
No—no tears! You *be* the tears! Hey, you there
by the strobe light—get that puffier squirrel, yeah,
that one, good—and make him a little hat to wear
from one of the paper cups at the water dispenser, okay?
Yes, NOW; you're thinking, what, Christmas? One-two-NOW.
Estrella, pinch yourself. That helps the look I'm going for.
What, "where"? On your cheek, on that pillowy ass,
who cares, it should show in your *eyes,* like doleful tenants
looking out of your pupils and contemplating suicide.
You want *me* to do it? I didn't think so. Agatha,
you're the Designated Estrella Pincher whenever she waxes even
this close to gleeful. Now we'll . . . oh great,
stupid, you couldn't think to tie it onto his head
with a string or a rubberband or something? Do I *have* to
tell you *everything?* "Hi, I'm God, I just made you, now

I want you to start to breathe. NO
NOT THROUGH YOUR ASSHOLE STUPID!" . . . okay, see what I mean,
be independent-minded a little, there with your squirrel friend.
Ron, give strobe-light-boy here one of your chartreuse shoelaces
for the squirrel cap, please. Estrella, I . . . Ron,
I *said* "please." Okay. Good. Thank you. Look, I know
what I'm doing. I'd like you all on board with me,
a . . . "community." On the same page.
Listen, I'll tell you something . . . Augoosto, stop
with the Frankenstein clomp for a minute, I'm going to tell you
a story of how I got here, from when I was . . . oh, nineteen
about. In college. That sumer, I stole clothes from the laundromats.
Don't laugh! It was easy. People would leave them
spinning all day in those tumblers that look like
astronaut training machines. They'd get a latté,
walk the pooch, whatever, leaving me, *me*
and their drying, aromatic, susceptible clothes. I said
don't laugh. I'd sit there listening to the zipper-click, gallumphing
pursuit of a flock of chemise by a pair of painter's overalls,
I'd look at the lacy what-nots opening up
like delicate graceful lusty jellyfish: hoo-boy! But I don't mean
this casual thievery was sexual . . . I'd take a parka
as readily as a frothy thong. It wasn't economic:
I could afford clothes of my own. It was . . . well, how can a man
who has chatted with emirs and Pulitzer cockamamie writers
put it? . . . it was here a fluffing hoodie, there
a pair of jalapeño-and-sombrero-thematized boxers . . . and,
once I possessed them, I possessed the lives
behind them. I'd scoop them up with a true nonpartisan eagerness,
I was a Whitman, I was a libertarian, I . . . Maurice,
if I wanted you idly molding your gooey locks
into tiny prairie dogs popping out of your head
I'd have said so. All of you: quit your smirks! That childish snarky
pinpoint subcutaneous invidiousness will *not* do
this production a firefly-buttock's glimmer of good. Okay.

Are we quiet, comported adults now? Well, we'd better be,
you goosey palookas. Stow the squirrel in that gym bag for now.
Where was I? . . . Agatha, what?—for chrissake surely
you'll donate a stinking broken-down gym bag to the cause
of theatrical history. If there's even a *hint* of squirrel-doo
I'll buy you a new one, deal? Where was I? . . . okay. One day
I was at my hobby—not a "fetish," maybe a "compulsion"—and
after I'd snatched some jeans or a bra or who-knows now
a-hundred-and-ninety years later, I lifted a woman's jersey
out of that sweet warm lottery drum, a jersey, tattered and pink in the way
that told you it must have been a cherry-red at some time,
long before the use, and the need for thrift, with grease stains
on the front of it that would never erase completely if you laundered it
against rocks in a village stream for decades, and I held it,
I *imbibed* it, I was a vampire of its warmth, and I knew, I *knew*
how the woman who owned it was a version of that pink:
worn down from something louder and more attractive earlier.
I *loved* her. I wanted to *be* her.
Then you know what?—you, by the rubber rocks, if I catch you
rolling your heehaw eyes again while I'm talking, you're never even
serving fries in this city, got it?—anyway, you know what?
I was right about her. I say that for sure because oh god suddenly
there she was in the door, with a cop she'd brought, and I was caught
red-handed. Agatha, what? Just say it, if you can mutter it
to Maurice you can say it to me. What? Very funny,
"pink-handed." Now may I continue, klutzes and kvetchers?
Thank you. I was caught, and the cop was breathing "jail time"
all over the room, and I saw my tush in a downtown lock-up
mildewing there for lack of friend and finance, and . . . you've heard
of *inspiration?* Like a million little pickle-forks of lightning
from the blue, it came to me, and I said to him, "Officer, I'm
directing a school play. Really! I'm sorry! This is what we *do,*
we need to understand a stranger's life, and make it *real,*"
boohoo, boofreakin'hoo, etc. etc., and the woman *bought it.* The woman
believed it! She what's-the-word? She "interceded." It

worked. You know why it worked? Augoosto, clodhopper,
put down your hand: this isn't Blessed Sacrament second grade.
You know why it worked? Because (and I hadn't known myself
until that moment) it was True! I *am* a Director, and
this *is* What We Do! And you, my dears and doofuses,
my mollycoddled darlings, you can stand there in your solipsism
impatiently waiting for all of this foofoo jibberjabber to dribble
and die, but I tell you there are nights I've walked
the slipstream and the suckhole of the Sea of Doubt,
I've gone down to the edge of the Fires, insomniac, crazy for wanting
to know about life in its germ, in its animal howl, in its pitiful
limited human warranty, and I've looked up to the gods we've spritzled
in burning and rumpus across the sky and I've *been* them
for a drunk unsteady moment, I've seen the universe through
their omnifaceted eyes, and I've looked downward into the Valley
where the promise of dawn and the lingering fumes of rush hour traffic
commingle, and here I've taken to myself the entire
wraparound scene of false teeth, gun oil, shining coins
of orgasm as they're flipped through the body, cellphone zap,
Talmudic esoterica, small used-up tubes of anal lube,
our chopsticks and our logarithms,
prom dress, breath mint, angioplasty, taxidermied wolverine,
kachina doll of the pollen spirits, mistress of contrition
as well as queen of the midnight boogaloo club,
our swarms of hopes as they glitter and either fail or catch
and flame, our tiny turbocharged ambitions and our darkest
nests of intertwining fears, I've taken it all to myself
and been more than myself, or less than myself, directing
the Heavens, directing the Pit, can we do something
about these fucking squirrels in here, they're driving me crazy!
Who requisitioned these fucking squirrels! Estrella,
trust me: lighten up.

PAINTINGS,
POEMS,
SURVEYS,
SONGS, AND
OTHER LYRIC
FLIGHTS

Busy

How many poems have been written about the stars?
We've been busy, we human beings!
By poems I mean bridges, alchemical alembics
burbling with eggy messes, opera, rap,
orgasms, caesarian births, blown glass.
They all have their Keatses and Dickinsons.

One year I took an astronomy course.
The facts were amazing: so many light-years,
so much spectrum analysis . . . . But mainly
I drifted. I listened to the stars at their singing,
I fantasized that the craziest and most radiant
of them were the Keatses and Dickinsons

of outer space. Maybe *their* poems were about *us* . . .
even the kid on the corner waiting to lead a trick
up to his sister's room; even the woman whose income
is exhibiting **The 350-Pound Oyster!!!** for 25¢;
the scissors-grinder; the rodeo dung-cart man . . . unknowing,
or mute, or illiterate, or hidden Keatses and Dickinsons.

Song

If they had our backpacks, they couldn't.
Our spleen, our gazebos and bongos and penicillin,
the open book of our lungs and its doodled-up text,
our spit, our come-on gimmicks, our exo-robot arms
arranging cups of liquid radium . . . they couldn't,
not with baggage like that, our braille dots,
and our hail dents on the hood, our congressional records
squabbling climate change, and our red and yellow
plastic squeeze containers for the ketchup and mustard,
our Torah scrolls and our jellyroll blues
. . . they couldn't; the concept of zero,
even, proves too much, would torque it all
off-kilter, and so now imagine how absolutely impossible
with our unguents and our limericks and our guillotines,
and whatever those numbers are that we assign to the planets
of other-galaxy stars, and our foofoo curlicue poodle show dogs
(plus their ribbons), and the open book of our kidneys
where our joys and griefs are written in nephron tubules,
and our scimitars and our vespers and our nunchuks
and our obstetrical spreaders . . . none of these,
even in miniature, is possible, not our habeus corpus,
not our tortellini, not the filmy chemise
with the two blue fleur-de-lys strategically placed,
and not the opening and closing book
of auricle and ventricle, our hundreds of miles of atomsmashing
gizmory, our God, our other competing Gods,
our hightop sneakers and lowslung jeans,
ixnay the waltz and ditto the pratfall, none of it
is allowable, not our first cries, not our last rites,
not our marrow, of course, they couldn't
with our hemoglobin and marrow,
no: there's barely
anything there in the bones of birds;
and so they can fly.

Migration Song

They have an interior compass
in their cells. The wild rumpus
of the deer halts, and they turn
to face a distant place they yearn
to be, then head there with unanimous
assent: it's part of what we mean by *animus:*
the bear, the eel, the pigeon possess
an original, geosensitive GPS
beyond our thinking. For the bee, "alive"
is arrowing back to the hive:
a bee doesn't "plan"; it isn't "science."
The migratory impulse in William Cullen Bryant's
nineteenth century beauty "To a Waterfowl"
is clear: the bird will rise like a high vowel
leaving the earthy consonants behind: it's time
to head for nesting grounds in another clime
a hemisphere away, and all of its aerial talents contribute
to the sleek completion of that pursuit.
This subject never grows dated:
Bryant's idea has migrated
over two hundred years, unloosed
from his language, and landed to roost
in my own small effort, here. And
—over oceans, over desert sand—
there are dogs that have been lost 500 miles or more
from home, and after weeks are at the back door
scratching for entrance. And the tortoise
journeys as perfectly as a mortise
pin through a mortise joint. The creeping
things. The whirring things. The joyful dolphins leaping
their parabolas in the waters of Greece.
Famously, the geese.
And the herring
is unerring.

Song: Lore

You ought to pray over the worms first,
on your knees, below a night sky where interior lightning
gives the clouds the anatomy of brains. Or the eyes
of several ospreys, hooked like cranberries
beaded onto a Christmas decoration—this is said
by the local venerables in a certain southern county
to be infallible. Try wiping the worms
in a benediction of lubricating oil.
Some say sugar them. Some say run them along
a vein near your nipple you think attaches grapple-like to your heart.
You ought to lay your head on the lawn,
mouth open, allowing the moon to glitter in there
like coins dropped into a wishing well.
Or count back from yourself to your mother's uterus
one scream at a time. You might consider using
a thimble of horse-jam scraped from an unshod hoof,
or sliced dried tampon ready to newly bouillon
in the water—these are said to be pungent
assurances of success. And what are the angels for,
if not invoking? What are your children's names for?
Some say turn in a circle thrice. Some say the oldest song
you remember ever hearing helps. Some say strict silence helps.
You ought to dip the worms in gin.
You ought to set six worms in the shape of a Star of Solomon
(if they'll stay in place). But the truth is, a catfish
is ravenous, is an endless small suckhole
of ravenous, a catfish will impale itself
no matter, a catfish is part of a world
that's *the* world—enduring, free of ideas of category
and consequence—and it doesn't give
a piscine fuck for our rituals,
our dice, our poems, the golden lure of our lines.

Tables

In religion—and this might be an extreme
example, and yet an example nonetheless—it's
when the supplicant kneels before the god the way
the wheat bows down before the wind, and then
that congregation writhes in a kind of pentecostal
frenzy, and a thrill runs through the stalks,
the heads are controlled now by a force
beyond their rooted, earthly lives and, given tempest-level
enough, they're taken up bodily into the air
and *are* the air's . . . it's like that; having lost
themselves, they've gained a place in something larger
than their selves. Evidently deities require us
to be mainlined into their systems. And I've seen it
too as Heidi kneels over the acrylically sticky panel

—18 feet x 12—she's dabbing ribbon and gearwheels into, making
art that in its turn makes her a component of cap-a Art,
enlarged beyond mortality into secular communing
with the silky, tendriled lily ponds through which Monet communed
with the eternal, as did O'Keeffe, and Chagall, and Turner,
all of them: magnified beyond death, all of them: made
a part of the immaterial Oversoul precisely through obeisance
to materials: their brushes and tins of turpentine and shellacs,
the bin of gearwheels Heidi fiddles with sacramentally,
the long transcendent river of paint to drown in and be
resurrected from. For some, immersion in the military.
Some, the thing—the one great thing—that happens
when the wings of air spank out inside your own lungs
with the first step on the conquered Alpine peak, and then

awareness of your smallness in its grandeur.
For Ricardo, it was Angela: we saw its start, that first night
when he met her on the patio out back of Café Russe, and every
gesture that he made toward her—a drink he bought,
a word he said, a word he chose to *not* say—was essentially
a genuflection. As for sex, her thighs held the pink chevron
of a higher rank of being, we could see he'd suffer
anything to be in its companionable graces: in a sense, to be
diminished there in order—this is the Zen of it—to be
empowered there. And of course she mistreated him. That's
the prerogative of a god, and that's the chance we take to glory
in the awe, at the portal. For some, their children; some,
their political cause. We wouldn't have the stuff of majesty
in us, without the other stuff: prostration. And so it was,

with Dominique Vivant Denon, who was one of the scholars
—one of the "savants," as they were called—who were embedded
(the term we'd use now) with Napoleon's 38,000 troops
as they battled, sleepless and starved, through Egypt.
Naturally the soldiers—brawlers, men of bloody action—
automatically disdained what they saw as the prissy affectations
of the scholars in their midst. The soldiers were insolent,
especially to Vivant Denon, "the lily-fingered sketcher,"
who was in the sands without a drawing table, please,
he said to them, please, come see this with me: the Temple
of Karnak. There is was: a building that could alchemize a common soldier
into the ethereal. And as one, they bent
to offer their backs. They made themselves into tables.
They made themselves into tables so they could be clouds.

Survey: The Lingering

We lay down tracks in snow, and so we know
we aren't ghosts. Light bounces off us.
Anyway, the sun's rays do; though we're no more
than bunched-up clouds, if that, to X-rays. I've seen photos
of supposéd ghosts more solid than my mother's lungs
in the image her oncologist obligingly tacked up
and backlit. Soon enough, the rest of her,
entirely, was no more than a chain of coughs
in darkness. Even so, I've never seen her in the way
that Arthur Conan Doyle witnessed filmy apparitions
manifesting, copiously in his later years, in the séance halls
in London, squeaking chairs and speaking oracularly.
"I have come from the far, far fields, my son. . . ."
England's gray with ghosts, is there an abbey
or Victorian hotel that doesn't claim
an ectoplasmic tenant? Someone once
asked William Herschel—this was after the paper
of 1802 in which he wrote how "deep sky"
also meant "deep time," and he was considered an eminence
of nebulae and comets—if he thought that we were visited
by the lingering shapes of the dead; his answer was only
a look at the night sky, and its dead stars,
and their radiance that still falls onto the Earth.
". . . the far, far fields." Doyle would have done better
taking up the telescope instead of the rapping table
and the Ouija board and the spirit trumpet oozing
lugubrious voices out of itself like a spouted oilcan.
In quantum mechanics, down (or up or contiguously)
in if- and non- and simul-worlds,
"ghost trails" thread the heart of the illusion
we call *matter,* and the quantum spectral presences perform
their alley-oops and alakazams along
those disappearing and reappearing ways; while in Malaysia
there was a plague of ghosts who wickedly caused
men's penises to shrivel; in ancient China it was common

for a family ghost to be installed in a wooden statue
—it would serve as the home's protector; and in Singapore
the ghost of an unwed woman can appear in a dream,
demanding to marry a living man—the stand-in bride
is a smiling waxwork two and a half feet high;
the ghosts in the *Odyssey* will congregate around
the freshly let blood of a ram and a ewe; in some
Greek stories contemporary with this,
the ghosts prefer fresh honey cakes . . . to every culture
and generation, its spooks. Celeste was still in mourning
eight months after Ronnie died when she discovered,
in a drawer of old astronomy lecture notes and older fountain pens,
his cell phone; and in turning on his greeting message, couldn't
turn it off: his voice—a simple, softly furred *hello*—
kept haunting her, until she drove in panic
(or it could be, as a tribute she wouldn't admit to?) up a country road
that same night, and she *flung* it from the car,
to a field below the posthumous stellar light
he'd spent his life observing. *Fuck it!*
Let the ghosts talk to each other.

Survey: It's a Small World

Globalism is yen is rubles kopecks ha'pence eurodollars
cowrie shells gold fillings hoarded in pillowcases oil
—as the vanity plate of the woman who owns the sex shop
says, ITZALLGOOD. But especially oil. Or better,
information—so the cell phone in a dugout on a wild spur
of the Amazon, and an e-mail portal installed on the 189th floor
of the Commco Building in Dubai, are equal zizzles in the datasphere
encircling Earth: an info-aviary in which we're each a squawking mynah.
My "50 Years with NASA" pin is back-stamped "Made in China."
As for the dead, they rise sometimes from bogs
with faces as creased as the linen of empty sachet bags
that we chance on in the backs of Victorian bureaus and uncrumple;
a mummified queen of ancient Egypt entered the Afterlife
with her mummified pet gazelle at her side and cuts of duck,
beef haunch, beef roasts, and an oxtail also
dried in natron and tightly wrapped in waxed cloth: hunger evidently
crosses the border with us, which is why one Chinese custom
calls for bowls of rice to be set on the ancestors' graves
as if on place mats; in the ground, a corona
of phosphor-glow will halo the skull, and maggots
weave the loom of the ribs . . . how different is that
(yes? no?) from the Zoroastrian "sky burial," where
the corpse is set on a roof and carried, peck by peck,
by vultures into Heaven. Or how different are the Viking chieftain
sailing into glory against the jet night sky,
his burning ship a torch sized to the gods . . . and the ashy plume
of her father that Tiffani launched by hand
from a butte in Montana, watching him wink
against the sun's set? Different. But global. Different
but everywhere and everytime and everyone. Another
Chinese custom is "burial money"—printed currency provided
for the dead, so they can bribe their way to a good seat
in eternity . . . so much of the "other" is eerily familiar, and
Unknownistan could easily be Oregon or South Carolina.
My "50 Years with NASA" pin is back-stamped "Made in China."

As for sex, because we ever-die—and even Methuselah,
Gilgamesh, and She undo to dust—we are (despite such aberrations
as the Shakers and famous celibate mystics self-exiled into deserts)
ever-eager for the hardness and the moistness and the roseate crown
of the body's royal family of pleasures. The woman who owns the sex shop
couldn't even for a minute address the history of the sacred
temple concubines of India and Egypt, or the flourishing
in seventeenth-century Italy of the gigolo trade for servicing the needs
of wealthy widows, but she knows what sells
(a brisk turnover, this week, of a vibrator called
The Coochi-Coo; and Blow Me, an oil that warms up
at the touch of breath: not oil in the sense of a petro-sheik, but
—on the scale of this business—very profitable oil nonetheless.
Of course the earliest well-known condoms had a global
aura: Sheik, and Ramses, and Trojan . . .) and she knows
"What Makes the World Go Round"—the name of her store,
its logo a planet Earth inside a hot, hot, hot-pink heart.
"This week, all goddam blushing newlyweds" including
a former-priest-and-nun duo, also another couple who met
at a funeral; "last week, all hos and strippers," and she shrugs
her ITZALLGOOD shrug. It was thus
that Set the usurper tore his brother Osiris to death,
into twenty-eight pieces that he scattered far; but Isis, Osiris's sister/wife,
did gather and then repiece the body, and did encourage
his manhood, and did straddle his manhood, and so
was he brought back to life. It was thus
that Kali danced for Shiva and the energy of their love
awakened the dead. It was thus that, in a famous unlocatable
paradise in the Tigris-Euphrates vee, the apple
was eaten, and the laws transgressed, and the fig leaves donned,
and death and commerce entered into existence, even as
the call of skin to skin, of loins to loins, continued
("hunger evidently crosses the border with us").
The ever-penis. The ever-vagina.
My "50 Years with NASA" pin is back-stamped "Made in China."

Survey: Unacknowledged Sex

Well . . . pollen. Pollen, obviously
(which is not to say *recognizably*),
as we travel through a powerful
gold drift of the sex of flowers.
It's like swimming through milt.
It's like chaperoning the party of fifteen-year-old kids
whose bodies insist they're ready for sex,
whose God and evolution and genome metronome
keep ticking sex-sex-sex, but no one, *no one,*
is allowed to admit this, everyone
text-messages or dances or sits uncomfortably
in a cloud of static sex electricity
so thick that a single errant loosed spark
from a carpet or petting the cat will make
the entire room into a bomb.

⌒

Those burrs around your pants legs
or the hem of your skirt: it isn't a secret
sex can be thorny and cling.
It isn't immediately apparent
that the heaving slug
is two slugs; that the tiny sucked-out insect
in the larger insect's jaws
is not just "food," but also
the used-up male; or even that the plastic bathtub duck
Mike Coleman left in his garden pond
"so that the surface doesn't completely ice over
in winter" was bobbing ferociously
[take closer look . . .] because a male frog
kept pounding his groin against it

—certainly confused about the who of this,
but going very adroitly about the amphibious how.

⁓

Some stories are funny, even the one that begins
with the woman one apartment over
screaming as if she's being murdered; you can figure out
by the title of this poem what the police found.
Other stories . . . it was funny
when one of the fifteen-year-old girls stormed
out of that party, having lost at a round
of charades . . . her newfound talent
at exhibiting pique, so sweet and so cartoonish . . .
and *not* funny when she stepped (deliberately?
we'll never know) in the path of a car . . .
in the grayish puddle of oil
and blood we could read the end of that story . . .
it turns out Sean from the high school football team
was part of the group she'd acted out
in front of, and lost in front of, and was
humiliated in front of . . . such an ugly example
of sex at work.

⁓

Its absence can't disqualify
its presence. So the bridge that spans the canyon
where a river was diverted, and thus carved
this slow gouge out of the planet . . . that bridge
in its vast accomplishment, and the fierce,
relentless zeal of that accomplishment . . .
is sex. The row of imposing heads
of mountain goats that line the study's wall,
the wall you first see when you enter the room . . .

is sex. Her ruthless scramble up the ladder
to the CEO position (the result of years of 24/7
machinating) . . . is sex. Whenever the high school
football team is playing crazy-hard,
a river is diverted . . . and it's sex.
A river is diverted, and a canyon is gouged out,
and into it all of the wars of the world will fall
and pile up, and still there's room for more and more
exploded sons and desecrated daughters,
more and more and more and more and more. It's sex.

*

And later that autumn, some of the fifteen-year-old
sons and daughters (a few sixteen by then) were sweet-talked
by a counselor into joining the "Teens and Abstinence" club
(although, as one opined, it might be "T and A" was *not*
a useful acronym), and so they took a pledge
to not have sex; and saw the pop-tune music video
To Not Have Sex; and read the books,
and moaned the prayers, and hiked, and biked,
to not have sex. And it was sex
and it was sex and it was sex and it was sex.

*

We know that's what it was in the flowers
of Georgia O'Keeffe; but try to tell me,
try to tell the genome of our species, that it wasn't diverted
into every fold of the rose
in that famous window at Chartres, as the building soars,
and our eyes soar with it, up to the glory of God.
And elsewhere, my friend Dora is eating out her lover
Rachel (*why* do guys get so turned on
at the mention of lesbian sex?), and Eddie and Dina

have put the kids to bed an hour early
by way of inserting a quickie
into their too-full schedule, and Dora
is lingering at the gateway and tapping to ask
for readmission with her tongue, and Annie and Frank
are in his mother's '97 Chevy skreeled over
into the wind-tossed shadows of Oak Hill Park,
and Dora the herd is running pell-mell now
through Rachel the open field, and Simone and Dante
are watching the instructional CD and lightly
stroking one another, lightly increasing the need,
increasing the need, they'll scream for it
at the proper moment, they'll kneel for it,
they'll set their mouths to the fount, and Dora
is so far into repetitive pleasure that now it's a wheel
endlessly turning, now it's a mantra, Rachel
is floating outside of her body, Dora is a flame
is a sky is a place where all matter is born anew.
And this is spirituality.

Survey: Frankenstein under the Front Porch Light

I'm from the era when "special effects" was a guy
in a rubber monster costume: sometimes
in a cheapo, shoddy, barely plotted movie
you could snatch a glimpse of zipper and where
the alien skin rucked up on the actor's shins, though
that example does disservice to the Creature
from the Black Lagoon, who went through nearly 80
changes of shape at the hands of designer Milicent Patrick,
adding up to 18,000 of Universal-International's doled out
1954 dollars. Over *200* pounds of foam rubber were used—expenditure
unnecessary for Riva Schmitz, the mother who,
with thorned switch and a simple lock
on her daughter's sour bedroom closet, posited
—to the courts, of course, but also and repeatedly
in the dreams of every child on my block—a brutal
monsterdom enough. I remember a doggie bowl
of water was involved, and also hat pins. By our later
Alien/Avatar era, megabeasts are micropixeled
—no one rolls the pea-green Martian latex legs on anymore
and superglues the Styrofoam excrescences—and yet
when the-thing-like-a-fisted-arm-with-shark-teeth
punches out of the spaceman's chest (i.e.,
it hatches in its host) the lesson
is much the same as ancient Greek mythology's
(Cronus, who devoured his own children; or the Furies,
Those Who Walk in Darkness: writhing snakes for hair,
and tears of blood: "as long as sin remains in the world
they cannot be banished") . . . *we're* the source of the horror.
Even Peggy Rabb, the sweetest poet I ever knew,
had a monster inside. So many kinds of this
one thing! Of Leviathan: "His teeth are terrible round about.
His scales are his pride. Out of his mouth go burning lamps,
out of his nostrils goeth smoke, he esteemeth iron
as straw." In Roger Corman's *Viking Women*
and the Sea Serpent, the laughable latter is a hand-puppet

fashioned of *papier maché*. Who would win the battle:
the wingéd elephant of the Hindus, or the wingéd bull
of the Babylonians? Burr-Woman "climbs upon the hero's back
and can't be dislodged, until he dies of fatigue."
King Kong's armatured model was only eighteen inches tall
(sponge, lambskin, rubber). Fire-Moccasins sets everything on flame
with his eponymous footwear. Gorgon. Medusa.
Yeti. Nessie. In Rilke the angels seem equally
horrific. *Even Peggy Rabb, the sweetest poet I ever knew,*
had a monster inside—although she, herself,
was its victim. It took twenty years for Emmy
—Riva Schmitz's daughter—to be arrested on charges
of child abuse, but it happened: inevitably a version of Burr-Woman
had been seeded in her, in her mind, in her heart,
and couldn't be dislodged. In 1956's sci-fi flick *Forbidden Planet*
the monster is an aggressively energy-crackling emanation
of the human id. *Yes, even Peggy Rabb.* The last time I visited
she was fed by tubes in her arms and through her nose,
and a five-year-old child who happened to pass her room door
screamed: a very low moment. On October 31, 1794
the optimistic British scientist Thomas Beddoes wrote,
"There is the best reason to hope that Cancer,
the most dreadful of human maladies, may be disarmed
of its terror and its danger too." *October 31. . . .*
Here they are, in the mist,
with their fists at the doors of our neighborhoods,
wearing our insides, out.

Survey: An Explanation of the Mechanics
of Her Marvelous Invention

She's seven. "The cardboard box," she says
with a bonsai-size but otherwise credible
imitation of pedantry, "is a time machine."
It has dials crayoned all over
its surface, ditto impressive
primary-color coils and levers.
She crawls inside.
            Meanwhile, a sudden, ambitious wind
disturbs the normally lackadaisical pond
in the forest preserve, until it confesses
its deeply secret store of catfish to the light of day.
Meanwhile, on Main and 17th, a busker's upturned hat
is reminiscent of a black hole: it could eat light
into nonexistence, all the way back to the universe's birth.
Somewhere we hear about in news feeds, in the steppe land,
tribal forces clash with tribal forces: some of the videoed weapons
are imported Soviet shoulder-launch rockets; some
are twisty blades that suffice
for leaving an enemy's head just loosely dangling
by a single strip of skin (or an enemy's child's head)
and go back in this same design for centuries, as the gods
whose Earthly primacy is being argued go back
in a recognizable version of their current form for millennia.
Meanwhile, none of this halts the traditional wedding dance:
the tiny silver ankle bells on the women that stand for
birdsong, and the beak masks on the men in a show
of caper and whoop that stands for bird fertility.
Meanwhile Magellan, Columbus, Balboa. Genghis Khan.
Joan of Arc. How many stars on the first American flag?
How many stars overhead as the Babylonian priest-kings
hunker inside their cloaks, against the chill on the top stair
of their ziggurat, and try to count the number of fiery thrones
from which their deities decree judgment?
Meanwhile the mammoth tusk some master carved

in the elegant shape of a pair of swimming reindeer
thirteen millennia ago. Meanwhile the small bronze figure
leaping, arched as purely as the tracked curve in an atom collider,
over the horns of a bronze bull—this, Minoan,
circa 1500 BC. The metaphorical river of time has slightly
defeatured these—moved them closer to general blur—
as surely as an actual river will smooth the information
off stone. Meanwhile an infant sucking his liquid portion
of a stream that runs back past the teats of an ape
and forward, outward, to some bioengineered mammalian
mother-figure nursing on a planet in the Milky Way
so distant we can't even imagine its soil and sky.
And surely there *will* always be lactation?
There will always be lactation—as long as there's us.
But who knows? Meanwhile the couple
sparking their sexual incandescence and honeycomb in the dark,
and the eerily slippery sound of sword-edge metal sharpening
on metal, and the night did descend,
and the morning did rise, and the people did gather together
at the shore and a wail did leave their throats,
a weather of wailing, a dirge, a song. . . .
                                        She

crawls out. "See!" How
right she is, nine minutes into the future.

O'Neill

And one—although they'd taken away her scissors,
and the silver barrettes like minnows
throughout the dark waves of her hair—still used
a raggedly torn-off fingernail to cut
a row of mysterious birdtracks and herringbones
up the inside of her thigh: it took
persistence. Another one climbed to the tower
and there pretended to fuck its bell, and then
remained on the rope like a pirate in rigging,
screaming out the names of his personal gods
nonstop for over an hour until
the intervention med team's tranquilizer dart
struck home. And one was so, *so* less
dramatic: she simply sat and rocked,
and sat and rocked, and wept.
It was madness, yes. Of course it was madness.
But also, for all of them, it was a language (think
the intractable conga-line figures of Easter Island's
rongorongo; or the infuriating and useless
familiarity that hovers about Etruscan writing,
of which we know only 300 words).
The lives behind Etruscan tombs remain
as sketchily understood as life on exoterran planets:
methane, silicon, insular.

The Phaistos disc looks something like a 6½" pizza
on which the circling around of peppers, mushrooms, and anchovies
are signs, punched in by dies . . . which makes it
"the world's first typewritten document"—from the Aegean
3,000 years before Gutenberg's Bible. There are 45
signs, the crested-helmet warrior,

the bare-breasted woman, the button (shield?), the fish,
the runner, the flying bird with (it looks like) a tampon
dangling from its underside by a string, the standing bird,
the shape that looks to me like a catcher's mitt, the "pagoda,"
the "paddle," the "whisk," the "rain pocks," the "speculum". . . .
These are arranged on the fired clay surfaces
(both sides: here, my pizza analogy fails) into 61 groups,
a script that, since its discovery in Crete in 1908,
has not been found on even a single other artifact,
and can't be linked to any language, and thus
is undecipherable. As you might imagine, that doesn't stop
the assertions. It's a gaming board. An astrology chart.
A pharmacology formula. An alchemist's list.
The forgery of a rogue archaeologist. "Powerful
kook attractor," adds the scholar Jacques Guy, and this
is the point at which it becomes a navigational chart
of the original intergalactics who colonized Earth
when we were still sea-splotches fantasizing gills,
and over *here,* see?—where the "spatula" is next to the "floating boat"?
—their home world's coordinates!

3.

So many poets nowadays are solid,
exemplary citizens, with a CV
in a portfolio, and stocks, and a lawn,
and no arrest record, but you remember
the Famous Poet—this would be the 1950s—
Security had to remove from his classroom
capering like an ape; and then he'd return,
ashamed, but lucid again, and brave enough to stand
before that same class speaking Shakespeare
and Milton and Dickinson; and then break down
in a while, again, as suddenly and completely

as a card-table chair folds in; and then
return once more, from whatever
unimaginable place it was where they kept the mumblers
and flailers and mutilaters of chest-flesh
and those who heard God in the bathroom pipes.
And also the pioneer "installation artiste": she
said "When I hear the Voices it's like an actual
physical mouth in my brain," although alternately
with that condition she raised a perfectly stable daughter.
Is this why his poems and her art give out
such flares of genius we feel scorched, and somehow, then,
instructed in The Other Ways and The Mystery Paths?
—because these two are Rosetta stones
for us, because they bear the marks
of everyday neighborly language, as well
as—equally—the words that are spoken
in the brains in rooms where the lock gets turned
from the outside and you're suddenly alone with your hells.

4.

This statuary couple on the Etruscan sarcophagus
lounges in death, as in life, with an easy intimacy
and equality (Etruscan women kept their own names
in marriage, and they banqueted with the men,
which shocked their neighboring ancient-world cultures),
and the way in which they're carved from a single stone
enhances the sense we get of deep and untroubled
connection. And if only we could read more
of Etruscan, who knows *what* compelling details we would have
with which to frame the bronze mirror,
the terracotta vase, the great gold pendant
with a dog's tooth set inside? But lovers always speak
in a private tongue: as true for the couple

who live across the street from you, as for this stone
Etruscan couple who live across time:
the secret names; a hand cupping a breast
in a silent duet you're excluded from.
In fact, we're excluded from almost every conversation
filling the world. The fierce debate
between dark matter and matter. Songs
of chloroplast praise to the sun.
The final words of light as it slips across the event horizon.
Lips of wind on nipple of mountain.

5.

When my friend O'Neill [fake name] was released
from the institution, I picked him up
and we went for a beer—just one, a trivial transgression
from the doctor's stipulations. All the time
that he was in, he says, he listened to the thought-rays
of the other inmates: the man with flames
around his head like a lion's mane; the woman
who's a sorceress, as O'Neill could tell
by the signs her fingers ceaselessly made
like a stringless cat's-cradle webbing the air;
the kid who, when he wasn't restrained,
immediately returned to banging his head on the wall,
as if this were an announcement of what
his life was. And O'Neill understood them all.

I've read his so-called poetry: it isn't good.
And certainly I never care to be
inside those terrible walls, in that terrible air,
among those unspeakable rituals.
But just for a moment I felt ashamed
I call myself a poet.

1,000 (Exactly)

Certain painters might do justice to this overcast
—Turner, or one of the 17th-century low-country Dutch.

The clouds are muscular and melancholy,
as if a convention of sumo wrestlers is mourning a friend,

but even the dreariest funeral ends at last
and, when it does, a little razzmatazz of light

squinks out to land here at the riverbank
where, as I pass, I see my student

Lyle sitting, lost, as we'd describe it,
in thought, in scribbling his poesy into his notebook

that I've witnessed all year dull from handling,
going from an ebony leatherette sheen to a flatter

perfunctory black—lost, and far, a body
with its self beamed out to wander

through the myriads of worlds. As for the usefulness
of poetry . . . I can't say, can't defend it

in the way we could those actions with an immediate
and a practical application . . . someone changing the grease

in the deep fat fryer, someone punching
her birth control pill from out of the blisterpack foil,

someone glissandoing a mouse's genome across her laptop screen
with the thoughtless adroitness (although this quest

for curing bladder cancer might imply the highest of our callings)
of a chainsmoker at the casino running her sequence of lights

at the video slots. Adzes. Condoms. Brushes—from
the pinking on of rouge to the industrial scrubbing of vats

the width of a football field. There's a story of Albrecht Dürer,
who's already a famous artist by then: traveling

through Europe, he's approached by another painter: "Tell me
please what secret brushes you must use to achieve such verisimilitude

in your draperies and animal pelts!" . . . and Dürer says yes,
they'll meet tomorrow afternoon and he'll bring his case

of brushes . . . which he does, and when he opens it
the other fellow looks inside and says, "You must

misunderstand: I *already* use *these* brushes,"
and Dürer goes: "Ah." The catalogue of "surplus goods"

I received in yesterday's mail offers (among
the "Swedish Army Meteorological Kit" complete

with "weather balloons and precision barometer,"
"Mounted Roe Deer Horns" and a khaki

"Czech Army Parachutist Helmet") a small platoon
of sturdy-duty brushes—including a mushroom knife

with size gauge, tweezers, and (set into one end
of the hardwood handle) a "boar-bristle brush" that,

to the extent it says serious, tactile business
looks as if it could easily flick

the philosophy-minded Lyle off his rump and out
of this scene altogether. Lyle's so-called poems

may still be only imitative jumbles of the anthology pieces
he's read and, with a newbie's passion, loved

—they're sort of Piltdown Poems—but anyway
he sits there in a . . . let me call it *ferocious*

repose, in front of me but extragalactically
elsewhere, revolving his pencil point

in a cloud-thinned ray of sun the way
somebody else might turn a cigar around

inside a lighter's flame to ensure an even smoke.
You'd never guess from Lyle's abstract

contemplations that a world of weight
and of flesh in its range of abilities

surrounds us, but I might be aware of "brushes"
as a cue-word because of the headline

of the paper on the bench nearby, MARINE
REVEALS BRUSH WITH DEATH and, underneath,

a story of how the angel-floss we call the nerves
of the human body can relay pain

enough to fill a blue whale with agony,
hammer it crazy, beach it

to die. "I woke up in a pile of corpses,"
he's quoted as saying, "and if I hadn't passed

for dead when the guards went by, I *would* be."
Ten pages later the pleased engagement couples

smile like some very-well-remunerated lobbyists
for marital delight, and so implicitly remind us

that the body's expertise in pain
is mirrored by its connoisseurship

in pleasure. Those 17th-century painters
covered that range as they covered their home-stretched canvases,

just as thoroughly as our news feeds, only
. . . exaltingly. In one small oil, the artist's mistress has opened

herself for his delectation as fully as an oyster, and what we
might call then, by way of extending the metaphor, her pearl

is draped away from our sight by only the scantest
teal-blue napkin, everything around it

—from her ample belly and thighs to the afternoon
as it pours through the out-of-frame windows—

being a delightful tone in the register of peach;
and in a sequel oil, the two of them create

an eight-limbed symbol of indulgence, rendered
half in private under the half-attempt of a quilt

to apply discretion, although, also being in luminous peach,
it melts before our eyes like a butter

drizzled over the heat of their love. So that's
the pleasure part. The pain is there

in the portrait of a soldier—just some farmer really,
who's picked up a rake to try to defend the world

he knows, in the face of encroachment—bayonetted
and left for the dogs: a smeary cummerbund

of blood is dried across the torso, in a loud
diagonal slash that's like an accent mark

for every generation of human life that's ever been.
The pleasure/pain: that contradictory, inseparable

yin/yang has been inside us since our antediluvian
unicellular selves. And what I'm saying

is . . . what *am* I saying? I think
it's this: a parallel world has always existed

and always will, in which a Lyle is trying to write
about all of that, but necessarily needs to exist

in a single-atom-thin bubble-skin
apart from all that. The perfect image of this,

for me, is when a breeze uplifts the daily paper
and its headline woe, and skitters it

against Lyle's ass: he's totally unaware of it,
even as he's devoting himself to formulating

its utterance. Those 17th-century artists
might have nailed this for you in one swift look,

with a stabbing poniard-blade of sun-glare, with an ameliorating
poultice of evening shadow as it spreads

across our labored breathing. That's what their apprentices
struggled to master. That's our legacy

on museum walls, or duplicated in posters
and sumptuous "coffee table books." Still,

this poem is the picture *I* wanted to paint,
here, in a thousand words.

The Song of the Lark,
Jules Adolphe Breton (1827–1906)

The lobby was dark and deserted except where the night clerk sat behind
his desk with a science-fiction magazine propped open in front of him.

—Ross Macdonald

You've seen him too, his head atilt in a puddle
of Motel Cheapo oleo-yellow light, but his eyes
in the Alpha Centauri cluster. In Breton's
earth-tone oil painting, the woman is halted
suddenly in the middle of her day of wearying scything
by nothing we can see, or hear. She's truly beautiful
in a heavy way, as her life is heavy, her hours
of bending and lifting are heavy, the earth
she seems an extension of is heavy in the weave
of her skirt and the pores of her skin. And yet
the look on her face says she's transported
by something lighter than the sun-oranged air,
something outside of the frame altogether. A song,
from a planet other than hers.

ACKNOWLEDGMENTS

The poems in this collection originally appeared (sometimes with small variations in title or text) in the following journals, the editors of which have earned my deep gratitude:

American Poet: As the World Turns

Beloit Poetry Journal: Left Behind; The Clothes

Boulevard: Snow; Our Reference; Of the Generality; Silences; Lepidopteran; Street Signs; Dub; Benny; Song ("If they had our backpacks . . .")

Court Green: Survey: Unacknowledged Sex (as "A Partial Listing of Unacknowledged Sex")

Crazyhorse: Survey: Frankenstein under the Porch Light

December: His Creatures

The Georgia Review: On the Way (as "The Road"); The Stem; Smith's Cloud; To This; Oh; "The Pulses; My Personal Mythology; Two Brothers; The Neutron Bomb; Wings; 215 N. Fountain; Go Too; Doozie; Song: Lore; Survey: It's a Small World (as "Summary: It's a Small World"); Survey: An Explanation of the Mechanics of Her Marvelous Invention; O'Neill; 1,000 (Exactly)

The Gettysburg Review: The Song of Us against Vaster Patterns

Green Mountains Review: Lineage; Metonymy; Ong / Eugene / Monet (as "Radiation")

The Iowa Review: After the Broken Shoulder,

The Kenyon Review: Etc.'s Wife; The Point at Which My Wife Enters a Poem about the *National Geographic* Cover Story (November 2009) "Are We Alone?"

The Literary Review: Encyclopedia Brittany

Michigan Quarterly Review: Liquid; A Totem Animal; 22; The Story of My Life

New Letters: Song ("One essential difference . . ."); Secondary; Noon; Big Things (as "Diminutive for Grand"); World (as "Earth"); "What Would Darwin Say?"; Being Norman Dubie (as "A Brief Survey of Who"); "Try the selfish,"; "If you saw even the first rocket take-off for Mars,; The Song of What We See; Summary: Kinetic vs. Potential; A Gold Coin of Kumaragupta I (Minted AD 415–450); I Remember the Look of My Ex-Wife Sitting Quietly in the Window on a Certain Day; Migration Song; Tables

New Ohio Review: Deep Ink; Away; *The Song of the Lark,* Jules Adolphe Breton (1827–1906)

Parnassus: We Focus on Love, When It's Death; We Focus on Death, When It's Love; Etc.

Poetry: Keats's Phrase

Poetry Press Week (performance): Her One Good Dress

River Styx: "An isosceles triangle was the same on Earth or Mars."

The Southern Review: Snow and Air and Irving; "Who carries a telephone book with them when they are running from a war?"; Survey: The Lingering

Southwest Review: The Disappearance of the Nature Poem into the Nature Poem

Tin House: Jung / Malena / Darwin; Detective / Woody / Sci-Fi; Mapped

And some of the poems above were reprinted in the following:

Poetry Daily (online): Secondary; "The Pulses; The Point at Which My Wife Enters a Poem about the *National Geographic* Cover Story (November 2009) "Are We Alone?"; Liquid; I Remember the Look of My Ex-Wife Sitting Quietly in the Window on a Certain Day; Doozie

Comment (Canada): Keats's Phrase

The Rhysling Anthology of Poetry, 2012 (The Science Fiction Poetry Association): Kinetic vs. Potential

Motionpoems, 2014 (video): Jung / Malena / Darwin

No computer was used in the creation or submission of these poems, and the editors of some of the publications acknowledged above have earned extra thanks for helping me continue to be me; as have the staunch and patient and open-hearted crew at Graywolf Press, especially Fiona McCrae, Jeff Shotts, Katie Dublinski, Marisa Atkinson, and Erin Kottke.

Diane Boller, Stephen Corey, Don Selby, Bob Stewart: you're doozies!

Albert Goldbarth has been publishing books of note for forty years, including *The Kitchen Sink: New and Selected Poems 1972–2007,* which was a finalist for the *Los Angeles Times* Book Prize and received the Bingham University Milt Kessler Award. Among other honors, he has twice won the National Book Critics Circle Award in poetry, and has received a Guggenheim Fellowship, three fellowships from the National Endowment for the Arts, and the Poetry Foundation's Mark Twain Award. In addition to his poetry, Goldbarth is the author of five collections of essays, including *Many Circles: New and Selected Essays,* and a novel, *Pieces of Payne.* He lives in Wichita, Kansas.

Book design by Rachel Holscher. Composition by Bookmobile Design & Digital Publisher Services, Minneapolis, Minnesota. Manufactured by Versa Press on acid-free, 30 percent postconsumer wastepaper.